LEAF SUPPLY

LEAF

A GUIDE TO KEEPING HAPPY HOUSEPLANTS

SUPPLY

Lauren Camilleri + Sophia Kaplan

Smith
Street
Books

CONTENTS

INTRODUCTION

AS URBAN DWELLERS, many of us live in high-density areas and crave a connection with our natural environment. With limited access to green spaces, bringing the outside in can satisfy our desire to be close to nature. Whether filling our spaces with lush greenery or assembling an exciting array of cacti, indoor plants can have an amazing impact on our lives. Softening hard surfaces and providing visually stunning displays, plants elevate merely stylish interiors to places where we can take refuge and be rejuvenated.

We may be biased, but it's safe to say we think plants are pretty damn incredible and we're huge believers that spaces filled with greenery are the best places to inhabit. There is an enduring attraction that goes well beyond the aesthetic; plants are living things that continually grow and evolve. The act of caring for and tending to an indoor garden is immensely rewarding. Watching new leaves unfurl on a healthy and thriving plant seriously floats our boat.

Even better, there's plenty of scientific proof that plants do us good. NASA's Clean Air Study suggests that many common indoor plants are capable of detoxifying the air in our spaces. They naturally remove toxic agents, such as formaldehyde and benzene, that are given off by paints, glues and everyday household items. Turning carbon dioxide into oxygen improves air quality and provides higher oxygen levels that can have positive effects on our health and well-being. Other studies indicate that productivity and creativity can also be improved with the addition of plants. Basically, plants make people happy!

We started Leaf Supply with the simple aim of spreading our love for plants. We wanted to give people the information and tools needed to bring a little nature into their homes. We also wanted to open people's eyes to more unusual varieties of indoor plants and share our knowledge of hard-to-find gems for those fellow plant

> PLANTS MAKE PEOPLE HAPPY AND WE'RE HUGE BELIEVERS THAT SPACES FILLED WITH GREENERY ARE THE BEST PLACES TO INHABIT

—

> PLANTS BRING CLEAN AIR, BEAUTY AND LIFE TO A SPACE. THE LUSH FOLIAGE OF A BOSTON FERN (*NEPHROLEPSIS EXALTATA*) OR RUBBER PLANT (*FICUS ELASTICA*) WILL HELP TO SOFTEN HARSH EDGES AND DRESS UP WHITE WALLS AND JOINERY.

fanatics out there. This book is the culmination of these aims, and we're excited to share our experiences of the joys of living with plants.

The variety of indoor plants available these days is extensive: from more traditional palms and philodendrons to unusual alocasia and air plants. In this book, we'll explore these and plenty in between. There's a plant out there for everyone and every space, and we want to help you find it. We'll walk you through leafy tropical plants, succulents and cacti, along with some rarer specimens, and we hope this inspires you to either begin or expand your indoor jungle.

Many people lack confidence when it comes to keeping indoor plants. There's no doubt the fear of killing plants has dissuaded many a hopeful gardener from what is an amazingly rewarding pursuit. The idea that some people are cursed with a black thumb is nonsense. Armed with the right knowledge, anyone is capable of keeping a plant alive and we're here to help. Our Living with Plants chapter will prime you with the tips and tricks you need to not only sustain an indoor garden but to allow it to flourish.

We love a good stickybeak as much as the next person, and in researching and photographing this book we were kindly invited into the plant-filled spaces of some fellow plant lovers. In our Plant People sections you'll get a peek inside too – a chance to see the creative ways individuals incorporate plants into their homes and work spaces. These insights into the connections people have with their plants and how they affect their lives will hopefully stir even the most novice of indoor gardeners to adopt a green friend.

By the end of this book we hope that you come to appreciate plants on a whole new level. As you marvel at their shapes, structure, textures and colours, and learn to care for them and how to group and style them using different pots and props, you can transform your little piece of the world into a greener, healthier and more vibrant space. Let's get greening, folks!

∧ IS THERE ANYTHING CUTER THAN A TODDLER WITH A TODDLER-SIZED SWISS CHEESE PLANT (MONSTERA DELICIOSA)?
‹ PLANT SHELFIES ARE DEFINITELY A THING, SO FILL YOUR SHELVES WITH GREENERY (AND PLANT BOOKS) AND POST TO INSTAGRAM STAT!

IT'S IMPORTANT TO REMEMBER THAT even the hardiest of plants are living things that need care and attention to keep them happy and healthy. In this section, we'll talk you through the basics: water, light, temperature, humidity, soil and fertiliser, and how to select the right pot. Armed with the basics, we hope you will have the confidence to grow a thriving indoor jungle and become the plant parents you were destined to be.

WHERE TO START

There are a couple of factors you need to consider before purchasing your first indoor plants. The absolute best way to ensure a happy and healthy indoor plant is to make sure it gets the light it needs to thrive. If you're desperate for a cactus but your living room is devoid of any natural light you're going to end up with one very sad-looking prickle. Save any sun worshippers, such as cacti or a Bird of paradise for the windowsill or a sunny balcony.

It's important to consider the environment of your home. Do you live in a tropical climate? Or somewhere more crisp and cool? How much light do different parts of your home receive? Are you an attentive plant parent or someone who maybe forgets about the little guys every now and then? Trust us, there's a plant for all of these scenarios.

PRIME POSITION

Once you've assessed the light and temperature conditions of your space, it's time to work out exactly where your new foliage will go. Your chosen space will affect the size and shape of the plant you'll be looking for. If you've got some shelves calling out for a little green attention, you might choose a trailing plant that cascades down towards the ground. Or perhaps you have a neglected corner that's perfect for a larger statement plant.

In any case it's time to get inspired. These pages are filled with gorgeous green spaces, ideas for displaying and styling indoor plants and plenty of plant profiles to help you pick out the perfect foliage for building your indoor jungle. Look to magazines, search the interwebs and scope out your friends' houses; greenspiration is really all around.

THE ABSOLUTE BEST WAY TO ENSURE A HAPPY AND HEALTHY INDOOR PLANT IS TO MAKE SURE IT GETS THE LIGHT IT NEEDS TO THRIVE

TIME TO SHOP

So, you've decided on the plant of your dreams and now it's time to track it down. Head to your local nursery and check out some of the foliage in the flesh. You may have a particular plant in mind, but it's also good to see what's looking its absolute best. Glossy, vibrant leaves, fullness in shape and fresh leaf growth are all signs of a super-healthy plant. Opting for anything that looks less than perfect will potentially lead to heartache down the road.

HOME TIME

It's exciting to finally get your new plant purchases home, and it can be very tempting to introduce them to their green siblings as soon as possible. However, hold fire. It's best to give any new plants a short period in quarantine to ensure that there are no pests or diseases lurking that could spread to your other plants. It's important to provide the same conditions the plant will have in its chosen spot, and try and get into a regular watering schedule from the get-go. It's not uncommon for plants to experience a level of stress from being moved to a new location. Leaving the luxury of a greenhouse where they are enjoying prime growing conditions and being subjected to lower light and humidity levels than they're used to can cause some initial leaf loss. Don't be too concerned if a few of the lower leaves drop off, but if this persists it may be that the spot you've chosen isn't giving your plant the right conditions it needs to thrive. Plants generally like to remain in one spot, but don't be afraid to shift them around until you find the place where they can live their best life.

Once your plant is set up, it's probably only now that the responsibility of caring for this precious piece of foliage really starts to sink in, along with, potentially, a bit of panic. But trust us, you've got this! Read on plant parents, and you will be armed with all that you need to know to enjoy a long and happy life with your new plant family!

‹ IT'S IMPORTANT TO THINK ABOUT WHAT POTS YOU'LL BE USING WHEN CHOOSING YOUR PLANTS. WILL THEY HAVE BOOBS ON THEM IS ANOTHER BIG QUESTION WORTH ASKING!
⌄ HANGING PLANTS CASCADING FROM THEIR POTS LOOK FANTASTIC AGAINST A WINDOW.

^ CHIC TOOLS MAKE FOR EXTRA-HAPPY PLANTS! PLUS THEY LOOK THE BIZ, TOO. < SET ASIDE ONE DAY EACH WEEK TO WATER YOUR PLANTS, BUT DON'T FORGET TO CHECK IN WITH THEM REGULARLY TO MAKE SURE THEIR NEEDS ARE BEING MET.

SOIL + FERTILISER

THIS IS ALWAYS a good place to start as it's where the seed or the propagated roots of your plant will spring from. Soil is a vital element for ensuring our indoor plants thrive. It stores water and nutrients for the plant's roots, while providing adequate drainage so that the plant doesn't get waterlogged. It also facilitates air circulation so that the roots have access to oxygen.

It's worth noting that even though it's often referred to as soil, most commercially produced potting mix doesn't contain any actual soil, but is rather a mix of organic and inorganic matter, often enriched with fertiliser. Peat moss tends to be the base of many bagged potting mixes as it adds lightness to a mix and improves water retention. Plants that like moist soil, such as ferns and begonias, will generally do well in a peat moss-based mix that retains moisture.

Desert-dwelling creatures, such as many cacti and succulents, prefer a drier home. The best soil for cacti and succulents is a coarse and sandy potting mix. This is because these guys prefer big drinks of water less frequently, as they harvest moisture quickly and store it in their succulent bodies. It's important that any excess water can drain away easily to avoid the plant taking on too much liquid or the roots sitting in damp soil.

Whatever you're planting, before potting it's important to consider the relationship your plant will have with its soil.

SOME USEFUL TERMS

SOIL A combination of inorganic particles of various sizes mixed with organic material at various stages of decomposition.

PH The measure of acidity or alkalinity in the soil, measured on a scale of 0 to 14. The pH of a soil affects the performance of the plants growing in it.

VERMICULITE An inorganic mineral which increases drainage and aeration. It also helps to retain water and valuable nutrients.

PERLITE An inorganic component in soil that increases aeration and drainage.

PEAT MOSS A spongy material mined from peat bogs (which are the results of organic matter decomposing over thousands of years below the ground). It drains well but holds a large amount of moisture. It's used in combination with sand for propagation and in potting mix.

SPHAGNUM MOSS This moss has longer fibres than peat moss. It is used for orchid mixes and for lining hanging baskets.

PROPAGATING SAND A very coarse, washed sand (almost a gravel, but free from fine particles). This is the same material as aquarium sand, also sometimes called coarse sand, river sand or washed granitic sand. It is used extensively in propagating seeds and cuttings, and is usually mixed with peat or vermiculite.

SAND Often added to potting mixes to speed up drainage. Because coarse sand cannot hold moisture well, a sandy mix will dry out quickly, which is ideal for cacti and succulents that prefer water in small gulps. It's important to use horticultural or washed sand that is free from salt and other impurities.

ACTIVATED CHARCOAL Neutralises soil by removing the acids. The process of activation makes it more porous and, hence, more absorbent. Charcoal is great at absorbing and removing any nasty smells that wet soil can produce. Layered in the bottom of pots and containers, it can provide extra drainage and has antibacterial properties.

VERMICULITE

PEAT MOSS

ACTIVATED CHARCOAL

PERLITE

SAND

PLANT FOOD

Plants are nourished and energised by sunlight, but they get their minerals from air, water and potting mix. Many indoor plants are low maintenance, so it's not always essential to fertilise them, and many plants will get along just fine without it. Having said that, fertiliser can support and encourage growth, giving your indoor greenery a bit of a boost. It's important to get the timing and quantities correct to avoid over-fertilising, which can lead to issues such as leaf burn. Here are some tips to help you get it right.

Plants require three key elements for healthy growth and luscious foliage: nitrogen (N), phosphorus (P) and potassium (K). Generally, fertilisers rich in nitrogen will excite healthy growth and green in your foliage, while those with a higher phosphorus content will ensure your flowering plant pal blooms at its best. Potassium helps your plant to build up its supplies for the winter months. For the majority of your leafy houseplants, a fertiliser rich in nitrogen with decent levels of phosphorus and potassium will be all you need to keep your plants looking beautiful and lush.

Liquid and slow-release fertilisers are best for indoor plants. When using liquid fertiliser, err on the side of caution and dilute it slightly more than the instructions specify to ensure you don't burn the leaves of your favourite indoor plants. You can always increase the amount down the track. Slow-release fertilisers compress nutrients into hard-to-dissolve pellets that are sprinkled onto the soil and will feed plants over a sustained period of time. It's preferable to fertilise your plants during their active growing periods, as this is when they are most able to process and utilise the extra nutrients. Limiting fertilising to these times allows plants to have a much-needed break in the colder months. Try to use organic fertilisers wherever possible, and always keep plants with added fertiliser away from children and pets.

FERTILISER CAN SUPPORT AND ENCOURAGE GROWTH, GIVING YOUR INDOOR GREENERY A BIT OF A BOOST

SOIL CARE KEY

Where possible, use quality, organic potting mix specifically formulated for individual plant types.

Well-draining Water is able to drain easily via the addition of vermiculite or perlite, which increases aeration while retaining valuable nutrients.

Moisture-retaining A potting mix that retains moisture with the inclusion of peat or compost.

Coarse + sandy A potting mix with a high content of sand and grit, which allows water to quickly drain away from roots. Perfect for desert dwellers.

WATER

WHEN IT COMES TO PLANT CARE one of the biggest mistakes people make is overwatering. It's so easy to kill your precious plants with kindness!

One important thing to understand is that a plant's water needs are closely related to the amount of light it receives. It's about striking a balance between the light and water your plants take in. Generally, the more light absorbed, the greater the growth and the more water is needed. The seasons will also affect this balance and in the cooler months, when light and temperature is lower and your plants are in their dormant period, you will find less water is required.

There are many variables which make it difficult to suggest exactly how often a plant should be watered. While many foliage plants will be content with a good soaking once a week, it's vital to check in with your plants regularly to make sure your watering schedule is meeting their needs. Get into the habit of looking over these plants every 3–4 days to assess where they're at.

When watering foliage plants, it's best to let the soil dry out between waterings so that the roots don't become waterlogged. To check if your plant is thirsty, simply stick your finger in the potting mix toward the edge of the container – if the first 5 cm (2 in) of soil is dry, it's time for a water. Gently lift your plant's foliage and flood the potting mix with tepid water until a trickle appears from the drainage hole at the bottom. Let the plant soak up the water for 30 minutes, then empty any remaining water from the saucer. It's often a good idea to water these plants in the shower or outside, so the excess water can drain away easily.

For succulents and cacti, the watering needs are very different. These guys need to be watered much less frequently as they store water in their succulent leaves. A lot of people make the mistake of spritzing or misting their succulents, but the most effective way to water them is to directly soak the soil with a hose or watering can, then let it dry out completely before any more water is given. Fortnightly to monthly watering should do the trick for these plants, particularly if the weather is humid. During their dormant period in the colder months, watering can be reduced even further.

> A WATERING CAN WITH A THIN SPOUT PROVIDES PRECISION WHEN WATERING SMALLER POTTED PLANTS.
⌄ GATHERING LARGER PLANTS IN THE SHOWER ON WATERING DAY SAVES TIME AND ALLOWS YOU TO WATER PLANTS THOROUGHLY WHILE ALLOWING EXCESS WATER TO DRAIN AWAY.

LIQUID GOLD

It's safe to say that most of us water our plants with water straight from the tap. Generally, this shouldn't cause too much trouble, but for some plants, however, this can be a bit of a hazard. Tap water – depending on its source, usually contains a mix of salt and minerals that can build up in soil and potentially inhibit the uptake of nutrients and thus reduce your plants' growth and health. The absolute best water for our foliage friends is the glorious liquid that falls from the sky; so when grey clouds are overhead, get your plants outside and let them soak up the rain.

For those of us living in inner-city apartments it's not always possible to get your plants outside so a clever trick is to let tap water sit in a watering can or bucket for at least 24 hours before watering. This allows any chlorine or fluoride to dissipate, so you'll have a batch of chlorine-free water ready to go the next time you give your plants a drink. The exception to this are carnivorous plants as they are more sensitive and should always be watered with rain water or deionised/distilled water.

WATER CARE KEY

Dipping your finger regularly in the top layer of soil is the best way to monitor the watering needs of your plants. Note that seasonal differences will effect watering frequency, and you will generally need to reduce watering in the cooler months.

Low Water roughly once a fortnight or when the majority of the soil has dried out.

Moderate Water roughly once a week when the first 5 cm (2 in) of soil has dried out.

High Water roughly twice a week when the soil surface has dried out.

Misting Spritz your plants using a spray bottle filled with water once a week or so, to increase humidity levels.

LIGHT + TEMP

AS A GENERAL RULE, plants need light to live. Through the process of photosynthesis, plants use light along with water and carbon dioxide to create their food and release oxygen into the air. Of course, different plants require different levels of light, and picking a spot with the right light requirements will help to keep them happy.

Each of the plant profiles in this book indicate the optimum light requirements for that species. These might include low-light tolerance, a preference for bright, indirect light or access to direct sunlight in order to thrive.

Most foliage plants and jungle cacti do best in bright, indirect light; that is, not direct sunlight that can cause their leaves to burn, but bright enough to provide lots of light interaction. When placing these plants on windowsills, north-facing is best. Keep an eye on the light coming in and ensure the leaves of your plant don't burn.

Desert cacti and many succulents are sun lovers and need the brightest light to thrive. A spot on, or close to, a windowsill that receives direct morning light is ideal. Even cacti can get a little too much sun, so avoid harsh afternoon rays wherever possible, or introduce your plant to harsher light conditions over time, gradually building up to a sustained period of direct afternoon sun.

Most flowering plants need more light than their non-flowering pals to kick them into bloom. Many flowering plants grown indoors will fail to flower due to much lower light levels than they would normally receive in their natural environment. Variegation, where leaves and stems are beautifully mottled with multiple colours, also generally requires more light. This unusual, yet often encouraged, mutation can begin to disappear if the plant ceases to get enough light, resulting in it reverting to its non-variegated state.

For those of us with a space that is lacking in the light department there is still hope. Opt for a low-light plant, such as a Zanzibar gem (*Zamioculcas zamiifolia*) or Devil's ivy (*Epipremnum aureum*), and try to give it a holiday in a light-filled spot when you can.

In winter, the sun sits lower in the sky, which means spaces that may have been flooded with light in summer and spring can become a lot darker. This is a good time to reposition some of your indoor greens to make sure their light and temperature needs are still being met. Plant stands (see page 61) give versatility to plant positioning plus a bit of extra height. Another great tip is to clean your plant leaves every month, either in the shower or by wiping with a cloth, allowing them to gain full exposure to the light.

> LIGHT STREAMING IN THE FRONT WINDOW OF LONDON'S CONSERVATORY ARCHIVES.
∨ A LIGHT, BRIGHT WINDOWSILL IS THE PERFECT SPOT FOR A PERUVIAN OLD MAN CACTUS (*ESPOSTOA LANATA*) TO SOAK UP THE RAYS.

HOT + STEAMY

As the seasons change you need to pay close attention to the humidity and temperature of your indoor spaces as these can affect how your plants survive throughout the year. Humidity relates to the amount of water vapour in the air. Very low levels of humidity can cause a build-up of nutrients that can potentially lead to nutrient burn – those pesky brown tips on your leaves. Conversely, high humidity can cause a plant to hold excess moisture and be more prone to rot, fungus and mould.

As a rule, the thinner the leaf, the greater its need for humidity. Thick, leathery or waxy leaves, or those covered with hair, are relatively immune to dry air. Tropical plants, such as ferns, are humidity's number one fan. If you live in a naturally dry environment, ferns will make a happy home in your bathroom, as well as an exotic addition to your decor.

If your plant starts to get curled leaves and dry leaf tips, it may be because the air is too dry. To create more humidity, try spritzing your leaves every few days with a mister. It's best to do this with tepid water in the morning, so the leaves have a chance to dry out during the day. Sitting your plants on a saucer full of pebbles and water is another useful trick. This creates a moist environment around the plant and the pebbles ensure that the plant is not sitting in a pool of water getting a nasty case of root rot.

Another way to promote humidity is to group plants together. Plants release moisture through their leaves in a process called transpiration. By grouping plants together, you create a more humid microclimate that benefits all the plants. If none of this is doing the trick but you're keen to persevere with your humidity-loving foliage, then a humidifier might be your best bet. These bad boys will raise the humidity in the whole room, which should keep those moisture fiends sated.

Generally, the optimum temperature for photosynthesis is 25°C (77°F), but most plants will be happy at 18-25°C (65-77°F), coping with the occasional hot day and enjoying a drop in temperature at night. Dramatic fluctuations in temperature and humidity are the most detrimental to our foliage friends. In the cooler months, keep plants away from particularly cold draughts and avoid leaving them too close to heaters that can burn and dry them out, leaving them susceptible to pests, such as spider mites.

As you can imagine, most cacti and succulents (except for jungle cacti – see page 165) prefer desert-like conditions. So dry air and soil that has a chance to dry out in between watering is a must for these guys. For some extra help in particularly damp spaces, dehumidifiers will dramatically reduce moisture levels in the air. Ventilation is also an important consideration for all plants, but can be particularly useful for lowering humidity. Do your plant friends a favour by cracking a window every now and then!

LIGHT CARE KEY

Be aware that light conditions will vary from season to season. Reposition plants accordingly to ensure that their light needs are consistently being met.

Low–moderate Tolerant of shady conditions, but will also thrive in bright, indirect light.

Bright, indirect Enjoys a position that receives diffuse bright light; avoid direct sunlight.

Bright, direct Enjoys bright light and will tolerate and appreciate direct sun.

PROPAGATING

PROPAGATING PLANTS IS AN AWESOME WAY OF GROWING YOUR INDOOR PLANT COLLECTION ON THE CHEAP

—

WE ALL KNOW THAT PLANTS ARE PRETTY MAGICAL to have around, but even more incredible is that many can be reproduced via just a small cutting of a leaf, stem or root. Surely we're not the only ones guilty of swiping a small cutting or two from a thriving succulent in a stranger's front garden? Sharing is caring and the truth is, propagating plants is an awesome way of growing your indoor plant collection on the cheap. There's something really lovely about sharing and swapping plants with friends. We have amassed an excellent scented geranium collection borne of friends giving away cuttings of every new variety found. Propagation is also a fantastic way of making use of bits you've pruned from a plant that is getting a little unruly.

An afternoon spent in the stunning garden of a friend's mum a few years back, resulted in a thriving succulent corner on my balcony at home. Succulents are some of the easiest plants to propagate, but there are many foliage plants that can also be reproduced with ease. We'll explore in detail the different methods of propagation as well as some tips and tricks to help you along. Generally, the best time to experiment with propagation is during a plant's growth period which occurs in the warmer months of spring and summer. Ensuring the stock or parent plant is in tip-top condition before taking any cuttings will also give you the best chance for success.

There are a number of different methods for propagation and the one you choose will depend on the plant you are hoping to reproduce.

OFFSETS

Some plants, such as the First aid plant (*Aloe*) and Mother-in-law's tongue (*Sansevieria*), form side shoots or offsets: little baby plants that pop up usually around the base of the plant. You do have to be very careful in handling and cutting these offsets to get as much of the delicate roots as possible, as this will give the new plant its best chance of survival. Carefully remove with a very sharp knife, then simply pot up in potting compost and care for it as you would the parent plant. Be careful not to overwater in the early stages when the root system is still developing.

Other plants suitable for offset propagation include the Zebra Plant (*Haworthia*) and Chinese money plant (*Pilea peperomioides*).

PLANTLETS

Plantlets are essentially miniature adult plants that are naturally formed at the end of branches or runners as a form of asexual reproduction. When the leaves and roots have formed to a decent size they're capable of living on their own as a new plant. Simply remove the plantlet and pot up using a standard potting mix with good drainage. The Spider plant (*Chlorophytum comosum*) is a perfect specimen for this type of propagation with a healthy parent plant producing lots of spider babies.

STEM CUTTINGS

This method of propagation is suitable for many common indoor plants including, but not limited to Devil's ivy (*Epipremnum aureum*), Swiss cheese plant (*Monstera deliciosa*) and Begonias. You have the option of growing these cuttings either in potting mix or directly into a vessel filled with water.

‹ CREATE YOUR VERY OWN PROPAGATION STATION WITH A MIX OF BEAUTIFUL GLASS JARS LINED UP TO HOUSE YOUR CUTTINGS. THRIFT STORES ARE A GOOD PLACE TO FIND UNUSUAL GLASS VESSELS.
⌄ THE SPIDER PLANT (*CHLOROPHYTUM COMOSUM*) PRODUCES PLANTLETS OR BABY SPIDER PLANTS. ONCE BIG ENOUGH, THESE CAN BE SEPARATED FROM THE MOTHER PLANT AND ROOTED IN SOIL.

Pick a healthy-looking stem and cut it on an angle with clean secateurs. Gently remove the lower bits of foliage and any other young growth that might easily rot. You want to let your cutting focus on putting down roots rather than growing leaves. Insert your cutting into potting mix or simply filtered water. Once it has rooted over a couple of months it can be transferred into your desired pot.

If you've taken cuttings from cacti or succulents, leave them out to dry for at least a few hours or a day before placing them in compost or water. This seals the raw edge slightly and reduces the possibility of rot setting in.

LEAF CUTTINGS

To propagate from a leaf, gently twist the leaf from its stem making sure nothing is left behind. Let the leaf dry out for 1–3 days to ensure that the cut scabs over and won't absorb too much moisture when you water it. Dip the stem in rooting hormone (knock off any excess if it's the powdered kind), and insert up to two-thirds in soil with the leaf pointing outwards. Gently press the potting mix around the stem.

Plants that can be propagated from leaves include Mother-in-law's tongue (*Sansevieria*), Christmas cactus (*Schlumbergera*), Zanzibar gem (*Zamioculcas zamiifolia*) and Jade plant (*Crassula ovata*).

DIVISION

You can divide some plants to make two or more. Species, such as Peace lilies (*Spathiphyllum*) and Boston ferns (*Nephrolepis exaltata*), can be divided into new plant pals. Early spring is generally the best time to divide plants and it's super easy to do. To begin, remove the plant from its pot. Place your thumbs into the middle of the plant, grab the plant with both hands and pull it apart. If this doesn't work, remove the soil and try again or use a knife to cut the plant up. Then simply pop your new plants in fresh potting mix and give them a good water. Over the next few weeks keep the soil evenly moist to help the roots take hold and heal.

∧ JIN FROM CONSERVATORY ARCHIVES AT HER PROPAGATION STATION.
< DEVIL'S IVY (*EPIPREMNUM AUREUM*) SENDING DOWN ROOTS IN WATER.

VESSELS

FINDING THE RIGHT
POTS FOR YOUR PLANTS
IS JUST AS MUCH
ABOUT FUNCTION AS IT
IS ABOUT AESTHETICS

SELECTING THE RIGHT POT

THERE'S SOMETHING UNDENIABLY BEAUTIFUL about the pairing of a plant and a handmade ceramic pot. The organic and imperfect nature of ceramics seems a fitting home for the natural beauty of indoor greenery. We both love styling beautiful scenes with our plants, and the vessels in which they are housed can play a pivotal role. There's an abundance of options when it comes to pots and planters, and each has its own opportunities and constraints.

Choosing the right home for your indoor greenery is not just about aesthetics, it's also important to select a pot that's the right size for both the root ball and the plant's height. To avoid having to re-pot too regularly, you want a pot that gives your plant room to move. On the flip side, moving a plant into a pot that is much bigger than it's current home can cause stress to the roots and the excess soil can lead to water retention and inevitable root rot. When re-potting, aim for something 2–4 cm (¾–1¼ in) wider than the plant's original home, so as not to overwhelm it.

Drainage is also an essential consideration, so it's preferable to use pots with a hole in the bottom and a saucer to collect any excess water.

The material from which the planter is constructed will also affect the care your plant needs. Take a look at the following options.

TERRACOTTA POTS

These pots seem like an obvious place to start when thinking about homes for our plants. From your bog-standard tapered flowerpot to more aged and textured varieties, there's a terracotta pot to suit every plant and space. The earthy, unfussy nature of terracotta works

really beautifully for housing foliage, and displaying them en masse in varying sizes and shapes is visually spectacular. An easy way to get that vintage terracotta look is to throw a few in the backyard or on the porch for a few months. Exposed to the elements they should get the perfect touch of fade and age.

There are a few things to consider when using terracotta pots: they will leach moisture from the soil, so your plants need to be watered more frequently. Also, depending on the thickness of the pots, the minerals from the water will eventually seep through to the outer surface, leaving a milky residue on the exterior of the pot. Although this may not appeal to some people, it can help add character and a naturally aged feel.

HANDMADE CERAMIC POTS

Thrown on the pottery wheel, pinched together by hand or manufactured on a larger scale, there are infinite varieties of clay and stone, patterns and glazes, firings and finishes. We love discovering local makers and ceramicists and all the new and wonderful ways they create vessels for our plants.

Handmade ceramic and earthenware pots are fired to at least 900°C (1650°F), which creates a pot that can be planted directly into. Unglazed ceramics will have a certain level of porosity, so some nutrients may seep through to the exterior of the pot, affecting its stability over time. Glazes provide a seal that will protect the pot as well as adding a beautiful decorative element.

PLASTIC POTS

When purchasing plants from your local plant shop, they're more than likely going to be coming home in the humble plastic gardener's pot. These practical but, let's face it, pretty uninspiring vessels, have adequate

TERRACOTTA WILL LEACH MOISTURE FROM THE SOIL, SO PLANTS IN THESE POTS NEED TO BE WATERED MORE FREQUENTLY

A LINE-UP OF TERRACOTTA AND HANDMADE POTS MAKE FOR A STUNNING DISPLAY. CHEEKY BOOB POTS ADD QUIRK AND ALLOW YOU TO HAVE SOME FUN WITH YOUR PLANTS. A DAINTY CERAMIC BOWL IS THE PERFECT HOME FOR A KOKEDAMA.

drainage and should be the correct size to sustain your plant for at least a couple of months before any repotting is required. Functionally, there's no issues with keeping plants in their plastic pots, but from an aesthetic perspective, you may want something a little more exciting for your new greenery. Double potting – placing the plastic pot within another vessel – is a super-easy way of hiding that boring plastic and allows you to dress plants up in beautiful pots without any stress to the plant. This solution is also an easy way to deal with watering as plastic pots can be easily removed and placed under the sink or outside for a good soaking. Any pot can be used as an outer cover for your gardener's pots, although it looks visually best if the plastic inner pot can sit snuggly inside.

Wrapping plastic pots in material such as calico or even brown paper is a great short-term solution for dressing up your plants, especially for gifting. Unless the pot includes a built-in saucer, the plant will need to be regularly unwrapped for watering.

HANGING PLANTERS

For trailing plants, hanging planters that allow all that lovely foliage to cascade towards the floor are the perfect option. They also help to create height in plant displays and are ideal in smaller areas where floor space is at a premium. Just make sure they've got sturdy hangers and that you're attaching it to a strong stud in the ceiling. Watering hanging planters can be a bit tricky indoors, so make sure you are able to unhook the hangers easily to transfer the planter to the sink for a soak. Alternatively, use a hanging planter without a drainage hole and include a layer of charcoal and pebbles in the bottom of the vessel to avoid overwatering.

SELF-WATERING POTS

These are great for forgetful plant parents, for people who find themselves travelling often and for plants that are positioned in hard-to-reach spots. Self-watering pots have a water reservoir system that you fill up, but much less regularly than conventional watering from above. They release water slowly and ensure that your plant's roots have a constant supply of moisture.

CLOTH PLANTERS

Indecisive? Love switching up your space regularly? Then cloth planters could be the answer you're looking for. From wild Ghanian prints designed by YEVU exclusively for us at Leaf Supply, to leather-look washable paper bags, these pot-plant covers are lightweight and super easy to switch around from plant to plant. Watering is simple: just remove the plant cover and place your plant in the sink or shower. Just be sure to place a small plate or saucer underneath the plant to keep the material free of any excess water run-off.

BASKETS

We love these for Nordic simplicity. They're also super-lightweight and a great option if you're not quite ready to commit a large plant to a big, heavy pot. There are also some great second-hand options out there, and who doesn't love the thrill of the chase, searching through vintage stores for something that's just the right fit?

KOKEDAMAS

Kokedama, which translates roughly to 'moss ball', is a type of Japanese bonsai that sees the plant roots and soil held together with moss and string rather than a traditional pot. They can be hung, creating a floating garden, or placed in a footed bowl or on a small plate.

INDECISIVE? LOVE SWITCHING UP YOUR SPACE REGULARLY? THEN CLOTH PLANTERS COULD BE THE ANSWER YOU'RE LOOKING FOR

REPOTTING

MANY PEOPLE FEAR REPOTTING THEIR PLANTS WILL KILL THEM, SO THEY PUT IT OFF UNTIL A PLANT IS SHOWING SIGNS OF STRESS AND ILLNESS

AFTER A PERIOD OF TIME in a pot it is inevitable that a plant will outgrow its home and need a bit more room to stretch its legs. Perhaps you will notice roots creeping out from the drainage holes, or that a plant's growth has stunted. If this happens, it's probably time to think about repotting.

Many people fear repotting their plants will kill them, so they put it off until a plant is showing signs of stress and illness. There really is nothing to fear, and your plants will reward you once they are happily in a new vessel where they can adequately access nutrients from the soil and water again. Repotting refreshes and aerates the soil and is best done in spring, so your plants can make the most of their active growing period.

Don't make the mistake of repotting a plant into a pot that is dramatically larger than its current home. Potting up one standard pot size is best (approximately 5 cm/2 in larger). Excess soil in an overly large pot can overwhelm a plant's root system plus it can also retain too much water, leaving the plant susceptible to root rot.

HOW TO REPOT
A PLANT

WHAT YOU'LL NEED:
- skewer/knife
- gardening gloves
- secatuers
- suitable potting mix
- a new pot
- trowel

1 Loosen the plant's root system in its current pot. If the pot is plastic you can squeeze gently around the base; in a solid terracotta or ceramic pot, you can run a skewer or knife around the pot to separate it from the soil.

2 Wearing gardening gloves, hold one hand over the soil at the base of the plant, then tip the pot upside down and ease out the plant.

3 Gently loosen the root ball. If the plant is badly pot-bound you may need to use a little force. It's not essential, but it can be beneficial to trim the root ball with secatuers to promote growth.

4 Add a layer of potting mix to the base of your new pot. You want the base of the plant to sit a few centimetres/inches below the rim of the pot, so let this determine how much soil you need to use.

5 Sit the root ball in the centre of the pot and use a trowel to fill in the sides with extra potting mix. Gently tap the base of the pot to help the soil settle, but avoid compressing it too much, as you want to maintain aeration in the soil.

6 Give your plant a good water and allow it to fully drain.

This process is the same for all plants, but repotting cacti can be a little trickier, requiring more care to avoid injuries. Using padded tongs or even rolled-up newspaper to handle prickly stems can save a lot of heartache and a potential trip to the emergency department! When repotting succulents and cacti, it is best to allow the plant to settle before watering.

EVERY INDOOR GARDENER SHOULD HAVE A COLLECTION OF ESSENTIAL TOOLS TO MAKE LIFE EASIER. CLOCKWISE FROM TOP LEFT: FACE MASK, BRASS MISTER, GLOVES, TROWELS, APRON, SCISSORS, WHITE OIL, SOIL WATER GAUGE AND STAKES.

TROUBLE IN PARADISE

WHETHER YOU HAVE BEEN a completely diligent and loving plant parent or you've gotten a little lax tending to your greenery, things can and will go wrong. When dealing with the natural world some things are beyond our control and it's important to learn from mistakes or mishaps. Don't get discouraged by a plant death, it happens to the best of us! Each experience adds to your plant knowledge base and will help you tackle any future issues that arise.

General plant maintenance is important for giving your plants the best chance to thrive. Checking in regularly allows you to jump on any issues before they completely take hold. Nipping these issues in the bud, if you will, may just save your plant's life.

Keeping leaves clean and free from the dust that accumulates can be done by simply wiping over leaves with a damp cloth or paper towel. White oil (also known as neem oil) is a good all-purpose spray to have on hand for spraying and glossing up leaves, and it can help keep plants free from nasty pests. Removing sick or dead leaves, stems or flowers as soon as you see them can prevent disease spreading to healthy parts of the plant, and allows the plant to focus on producing new healthy growth.

Observation is key with indoor gardening; not just checking in with your plants, but looking at the ways they respond to water and light, as well as noticing any changes in their growth. Plants are pretty good at communicating when things aren't going well and knowing what to look out for is half the battle. On the next page you'll find some tell-tale signs that things are awry and what it can mean for you and your plant.

> REGULARLY CHECKING OVER AND CLEANING LEAVES WILL ALLOW YOU TO SPOT ANY ISSUES BEFORE THEY TAKE HOLD, AS WELL AS MAINTAINING GLOSSY, HEALTHY FOLIAGE, SUCH AS THIS STUNNING RUBBER PLANT (*FICUS ELASTICA*).

GENERAL PLANT
MAINTENANCE IS
IMPORTANT FOR GIVING
YOUR PLANTS THE BEST
CHANCE TO THRIVE

YELLOWING LEAVES Older plant leaves may yellow and drop off as part of the plant's natural aging process and this is completely normal. However, if lots of leaves are turning yellow, including new growth, it is possible that your plant is getting too much light. Try moving it to a spot with indirect light and see if the plant improves.

LEAVES DROPPING This can be tricky to decipher as it can be caused by over- and under-watering, so it takes a bit of experimenting to work out which one it is. Regularly sticking your finger in the top layers of soil will tell you how quickly it's drying out. As a very general rule, when the top 5 cm (2 in) of soil is dry you are good to water again. Many foliage plants will let you know when they are thirsty by looking a little sad and droopy, but will perk right back up after a drink. Preferably you should water just before your plant starts to show signs of dehydration. Trial and error is the best way to get your watering right, so persevere until those leaves stop falling.

LEAVES CURLING This can occur when a plant is subjected to long periods of drought or low humidity. Try to water as regularly as possible and provide extra moisture by misting the leaves.

BROWN LEAF EDGES Dry air or underwatering are the major causes here. Another culprit is over-fertilising, where leaf burn can present as browning tips. Always follow packet instructions and err on the side of caution when using fertiliser. It's much better to over-dilute than the other way around.

WILTING OR BURNT LEAVES This is a pretty clear sign that your plant is getting too hot, and potentially burned by harsh sun. Tropical foliage, in particular, is easily burnt by direct sun and needs to be positioned away from windows where the glass magnifies the sunlight. Afternoon sun is particularly strong and damaging to many indoor plants.

LEGGY OR SPARSE GROWTH This indicates that your plant is not getting enough natural light. Reposition it to a spot with brighter light or a longer period of light exposure.

LOPSIDED GROWTH More obvious in some plant species than others, this is more of an aesthetic issue rather than one that can cause your plant any major damage. The Fiddle-leaf fig (*Ficus lyrata*), in particular, can get very lopsided unless regularly rotated so that all sides of the plant get exposure to the brightest part of a room. Try and rotate your plants little by little each time you water them.

ROOT ROT Plants with root rot aren't able to properly absorb moisture and nourishment from the soil, and will present as suffering from dehydration even though the soil is completely saturated. With this problem, prevention is definitely better than cure, and adequate drainage and a regular watering schedule are the best ways to avoid it. If the plant is salvageable, remove it from the soil and give the roots a good rinse. With a sharp pair of scissors or secateurs, remove the affected roots. Depending on how much of the root system you need to remove you may also need to remove one-third to one-half of the foliage. Dipping the roots in a fungicide solution will kill off any fungus that may be present. Make sure you wash the affected pot well with disinfectant or diluted bleach to avoid spreading the fungus to the freshly potted plant.

△ THE LOPSIDED FOLIAGE ON THIS UMBRELLA PLANT (*SCHEFLERRA ARBORICOLA* 'VARIEGATA') IS REACHING TOWARDS THE LIGHT SOURCE. ROTATE PLANTS REGULARLY TO ENSURE EVEN GROWTH.
◁ PROLONGED PERIODS OF UNDERWATERING HAVE CAUSED BROWN EDGES TO APPEAR ON THE LEAVES OF THIS MATURE SWISS CHEESE PLANT (*MONSTERA DELICIOSA*).

PESTS + DISEASES

These are an inevitable evil that you will have to deal with as an indoor gardener. Many plants bought from nurseries are already affected before you've even got them home, so it's vital to double-check your plants before buying them, and to look out for any signs that might indicate its sick. It's a good idea to keep newly acquired plants away from your existing foliage, to ensure that they're healthy before bringing them into the fold. Quarantining sick plants to ensure that pests don't spread is also advisable.

Signs of pests and diseases include:
- Leaves with brown spots, holes or nibbled edges.
- Insects anywhere on the plant.
- Powdery mildew or mould on the leaves, which can indicate a fungal infection.

Checking in regularly with your plants is essential for catching any issues before they take hold and do lasting damage. Pests and diseases will generally attack weak or unhealthy plants, so regular watering and adequate light can go a long way to keeping unwanted problems at bay. It's best practice to remove any dead flowers, leaves and stems as you see them to stave off fungus which thrives on dead plant tissue. Prevention, as with most things, is absolutely better than the cure. If your plants do fall victim to pests or diseases don't despair, there are plenty of solutions out there. In general, we recommend using organic pest controls and be sure to always wear gloves and dust masks when dealing with any chemicals.

COMMON PESTS

APHIDS Small, soft-bodied wingless insects that come in various colours. They reproduce rapidly and attack plants in clusters by sucking sap from the leaves and stems. To remove aphids, spray the plant with cold water to dislodge them or wipe the leaves with lukewarm soapy water. It's worthwhile spraying the leaves with white oil once they are clean, to prevent the aphids from reappearing.

FUNGUS GNATS Small flies that lay their eggs in soil that contains organic matter. You can notice them running across the soil and leaves, and crawling around on windows. They do little damage and are mainly a nuisance. It's generally the larvae rather than the adults you have to worry about. The easiest solution is to avoid overwatering, as the adults lay eggs in moist soil. Another good idea is to place a layer of sand on top of the soil, which tricks the adults into thinking the soil is too dry for laying eggs.

MEALYBUGS These nasty guys appear as small clumps of cotton wool. They are tiny insects that are coated with a white, powdery wax that sucks sap from the leaves and excretes a sticky residue which can attract mould and ants. The bigger bugs can be picked off with your fingers (wear gloves for this dirty job) while for the smaller ones, a cottonbud dipped in methylated spirits can be used to kill and remove the bugs and any sticky residue.

SCALE INSECTS Flat, oval-shaped insects that appear as black bumps on leaves and branches. They suck plant juices and secrete honeydew which ants feed on. Mature scale insects are immobile and covered with a hard brown shell. These can be scraped off with a toothbrush and then sprayed with white oil to prevent reoccurrence.

SPIDER MITES Teeny tiny mites that suck sap from the undersides of leaves and causes them to dry out and drop off. You might notice small red dots on your leaves and in the case of infestation, fine webbing across the undersides of leaves. White oil does a good job of suffocating these pests. Alternatively, if your plant is nice and strong, give it a high-pressure shower three mornings in a row to remove the mites.

WHITEFLIES Tiny white-winged flies that gather in groups on the undersides of leaves and feed on the sap and excrete honeydew. They flutter off in a cloud when you touch the plant. If they are affecting a strong plant, you can gently vacuum the flies away. Otherwise, spray with white oil.

COMMON DISEASES

Indoor plant diseases are generally caused by fungi, bacteria or viruses. Preventing the conditions that foster the growth of these destructive organisms is the best way to avoid sick plants.

Fungi is definitely not a fun guy to have around. It thrives in damp conditions and is responsible for a variety of issues including root and stem rot, leaf spots and mildew. To avoid these problems, keep leaves dry and provide good air circulation. Perhaps place a fan near where you keep your plants. The circulating air will decrease the humidity surrounding the pot and help the top layer of soil to dry out better. If fungus has already developed, it's best to start by physically removing the offending disease, either by digging it out of the soil or trimming fungus-ridden leaves. You can also increase the soil's pH level by sprinkling a small amount of apple cider vinegar, baking soda or cinnamon on the soil, making it more acidic and less hospitable to fungi. Failing that, you can buy natural fungicides at your local hardware store.

Bacteria and viruses can cause stunted growth, discolouration and foliage deformities. These nasties are spread by insects, such as aphids and scales, and, unfortunately, there is no effective treatment. The best solution is to quickly remove the infected plant from your collection and sterilise any tools that it has come into contact with using methylated spirits.

STYLING

PLANTS HAVE A WAY of completely transforming an indoor space. As you will see in the pages ahead, homes and work spaces come alive with the addition of plants. As a general rule, it's good to create depth, focal points and interesting shapes. Botanical styling is about being true to your taste and creating something unique, whether that's a wild jungle or something with just a hint of greenery. Play around, try different things and see what works best for you.

GROUPING PLANTS TOGETHER

Always consider the shapes of the plants you're playing with. Are they upright, bushy or trailing? What textures do the leaves have? What patterns do they make? How do the colours and variations work together? It's great to mix textures, colours and shapes to create a stunning vignette or 'shelfie'. Place lush leaves next to more structural stunners, ensuring that your plants don't sit in a straight line, and remember that uneven numbers are always better. Grouping plants en masse can have real impact, too. Think tall, short, high, low. Go wild and create an absolute jungle.

As well as looking the business, keeping plants with similar care needs together creates a microclimate that can provide much-needed humidity, particularly for tropical foliage. It's also easier to manage watering schedules when plants with the same watering needs are close to each other.

GROUPING PLANTS EN MASSE CAN HAVE REAL IMPACT, TOO. THINK TALL, SHORT, HIGH, LOW. GO WILD AND CREATE AN ABSOLUTE JUNGLE

FEATURE PLANTS

Indoor trees make the perfect interior statement, creating a lush focal point in any room. On its own or as part of a group, a large Ficus or Strelitzia easily takes centre stage.

ON STANDS

A great way to add depth and height to your plant displays is with the help of some well-placed plant stands. While beautiful in their own right, these accessories also provide flexibility in placing plants around existing furniture. From timber beauties to the more architectural wire varieties, you're spoilt for choice. Mix it up with varying heights, shapes and materials.

HANGING OR TRAILING

Varieties, such as Hoya, Devils Ivy (*Epipremnum aureum*) or Chain of hearts (*Ceropegia woodii*) are perfect for this. Group a few hanging plants together for a floating garden or cascade a vine down the side of a bookcase. Some vines will happily be trained to grow up a wall, or around a mirror with the help of a few small hooks.

DESERT PLANT WINDOWSILLS

Edgy and graphic, a line-up of cacti and sun-loving succulents is perfect along a windowsill. It not only creates an amazing silhouette but allows these desert dwellers to soak up some much-needed rays. Mix shapes, textures and heights for added interest.

PROPAGATION STATION

An easy way to add more greenery is to place your stem cuttings in chic glass bottles and watch them root. Unlike cut flowers they'll just keep on growing! And once they're ready to be propagated, simply fill your vases with a new bunch of cuttings and watch your indoor jungle quickly multiply.

∧ A SIMPLE EXAMPLE OF PLANT GROUPING WHERE THREE IS THE PERFECT NUMBER.
< THIS BOSTON FERN (*NEPHROLEPIS EXALTATA*) ON A TIMBER STAND MAKES A BOLD FEATURE WHEN PLACED NEXT TO ARTWORK.

AGE
NTS

TEXTURAL, GRAPHIC AND LUSH, foliage plants are the most prolific and varied group of indoor plants. From the delicate leaves of the Maidenhair fern (*Adiantum raddianum*) to the magnificent Elephant Ear (*Colocasia*), there are foliage plants to suit any space and climate.

Lusciously leafed statement plants, such as the Fiddle-leaf fig (*Ficus lyrata*) and the Swiss cheese plant (*Monstera deliciosa*) are highly desirable and for good reason; these beauties instantly change the dynamic of a space and are sure to draw admiration from anyone in their presence.

Trailing splendours, such as the Heartleaf philodendron (*Philodendron cordatum*), Wax plants (*Hoyas*) and Devil's ivy (*Epipremnum aureum*) bring a little jungle wildness to hard-edged surfaces, making them perfect for bookshelves and entertainment units. These plants can trail all the way to the floor or be trained to trail over furniture and across walls. They are also easy to propagate to add further depth to your collection.

Graphic foliage plants, such as Begonias and Peperomias, add texture and excitement when grouped with other foliage pals and can give your office desk a splash of probably much needed colour. If you're looking for extra bang, many varieties come in variegated form which adds further colours and textures to your favourite foliage. A mix of different textures, colours, shapes and heights provides visual appeal, so don't be afraid to have a play.

In this chapter, you'll find a selection of our favourite foliage friends, but there are hundreds of species and varieties to choose from to add to your collection. Once you get started, it's a highly addictive and rewarding pursuit – you can never have enough foliage in your life!

FROM THE DELICATE LEAVES OF THE MAIDENHAIR FERN, TO THE MAGNIFICENT ELEPHANT EAR, THERE ARE FOLIAGE PLANTS TO SUIT ANY SPACE AND CLIMATE

> FOLIAGE PLANTS COME IN A DIVERSE RANGE OF SHAPES, COLOURS AND TEXTURES AND LOOK AMAZING EN MASSE. THEY'RE ALSO FANTASTIC HOUSEMATES PURIFYING THE AIR IN YOUR SPACE, INCREASING THE GOOD VIBES AND INSPIRING CREATIVITY.

FATSIA JAPONICA 'SPIDERS WEB'

JAPANESE ARALIA

When it comes to impressive foliage, look no further than *Fatsia Japonica* with its lush leaves resembling a Schefflera (see page 72) on steroids. The variegated 'Spider's web' features leaves bordered with beautifully speckled markings that peter out towards the centre. In the right conditions the shiny, leathery leaves can grow up to 30 cm (12 in) wide. This plant is best paired with a minimal pot that allows the foliage to take centre stage.

LIGHT

Bright, indirect

WATER

Moderate-high

SOIL

Well-draining

LIGHT

Low–moderate

WATER

Low–moderate

SOIL

Well-draining

EPIPREMNUM AUREUM
DEVIL'S IVY

As Kylie Minogue famously sang, it's better the devil you know, and who could argue? This gorgeous trailing plant will delight with her glossy, variegated green and golden arrow-shaped leaves that can trail or be trained. The *Epipremnum aureum* is definitely one sexy devil. She does have a bit of a reputation for being easy, as she's a very forgiving and low maintenance plant that can thrive in low light. Not just a pretty face, the Devil's ivy keeps a clean house, renowned for her sweet air-purifying skills. In the wild, she can grow up to 12 metres (40 ft) long, but perhaps a little less inside! Having said that, this fast grower trails beautifully and provides some much needed lushness to bare shelves.

STRELITZIA
BIRD OF PARADISE

Known as the Bird of paradise for it's epic tropical flowers, *Strelitzia* make a great leafy statement in any sunny spot in your home. They like very bright light and can tolerate some sun – a windowsill is ideal. Opt for either the giant *Strelitzia nicolai* with its wider paddle-like leaves and white flowers or the petite and demure *Strelitzia reginae*, recognised by the more commonly seen orange flowers. Both will struggle to flower indoors due to lower-light conditions, but the foliage is so fabulous on it's own that you'll hardly miss the blooms.

LIGHT

Bright, partially direct

WATER

Moderate

SOIL

Well-draining

LIGHT

Bright, indirect

WATER

Moderate

SOIL

Well-draining

PIPER KADSURA

HARDY PEPPER VINE

The *Piper kadsura* is one amazing creeper. Originally from Southeast Asia, its beautiful, waxy green leaves will crawl out of the pot and right into your heart. Even better, this lovely foliage is nice and easy to tend to, so even the not-so-green-thumbed among us can reap the rewards. Trail from a shelf or plant stand to best appreciate this gorgeous vine.

SCHEFFLERA ARBORICOLA

UMBRELLA PLANT

Difficult to pronounce but a breeze to care for, the *Schefflera arboricola* or Umbrella plant is so named for its leaf formations that resemble everybody's favourite rain cover. This gorgeous greeny is also available in variegated varieties that can add pattern and interest to your indoor jungle. Keep in mind that too little light will cause the plant to get leggy and floppy, so a light, bright spot is best. If you're a little forgetful on the watering front Schefflera will cut you some serious slack, but a regular watering schedule will go a long way to keeping any pests, such as spider mites, at bay.

LIGHT

Bright, indirect

WATER

Moderate

SOIL

Well-draining

LIGHT

Bright, indirect

WATER

Moderate-high +
misting

SOIL

Well-draining

ALOCASIA 'POLLY'

AFRICAN MASK PLANT

When it comes to the *Alocasia* 'Polly'
we're talking about some seriously fancy
foliage. Graphic white on green markings
reminiscent of an African mask will add
instant cred to your plant gang. Definitely
one for the more experienced indoor
gardener, this stunner doesn't come easy.
High humidity is vital and getting the
watering schedule right is also key to
keeping your *Alocasia* thriving. Keep soil
moist but not saturated or soggy, and mist
the leaves regularly.

LIGHT

Bright, indirect

WATER

Moderate

SOIL

Well-draining

MONSTERA DELICIOSA

SWISS CHEESE PLANT

One of our all-time favourite pieces of foliage, the *Monstera deliciosa* is a design lover's dream. The glossy, graphic leaves along with the plant's ability to grow fast and large means this beauty is the perfect feature plant to spruce up your space. It hails from the rainforests of Central America, so it provides some serious indoor jungle vibes. Resilient and hardy, it doesn't take much to keep this plant happy, but being a prolific grower means it does need plenty of room to spread out as it matures.

Like most tropical plants, the Swiss cheese plant loves a bright position with lots of indirect light. It might grow beneath the rainforest canopy, but it uses those amazing aerial roots to reach for the light. A lack of light can affect the production of the holes in its leaves for which it is so famous. But also be careful with direct sunlight, as harsh rays can burn those same luscious leaves. To keep your Monstera in tip-top condition, add some liquid fertiliser once every three months or so.

The water needs of your Monstera will depend on how much light it gets. As a general rule, watering it once a week should keep it sufficiently hydrated. Give it a good soak, allowing any excess water to drain out of the base of the pot. Ensure that the top 5 cm (2 in) of soil has dried out before giving it another drink.

You also can eat the mature fruit – it tastes just like a fruit salad, hence its alternative name the Fruit salad plant!

TAHNEE CARROLL

Freelance stylist

⌃ DAPPLED LIGHT IN THE LIVING SPACE ENCOURAGES THE MOST ABUNDANT GROWTH OF TAHNEE'S SWISS CHEESE PLANTS (*MONSTERA ADANSONII* AND *DELICIOSA*). ⌄ INTERESTING CERAMICS COLLECTED OVER TIME FEATURE WIDELY IN HER HOME.

TELL US A BIT ABOUT YOURSELF: YOUR BACKGROUND, WHAT YOU DO, THE SPACE WE'RE SHOOTING YOU IN.

I'm an interior stylist. I studied interior design straight out of school and gradually made my way across to the media industry. I have worked my way up from an assistant stylist to where I am now. I now style large campaigns for furniture and homewares brands as well as major publications, such as *Real Living*. I am the co-creator of Citizens of Style, a photographic and styling agency that creates imagery and motion for brands, artists and magazines. I live in a two-bedroom semi in Sydney's inner west with my dog Rue, a Catahoula cross Border Collie and my housemate Cloud Tuckwell, a ceramicist who works at Mud Australia. Our house has a very eclectic mix of old and new; I am quite the queen of finding amazing stuff on the side of the road, but I also have a taste for expensive mid-century antiques and ceramics. The colour palette is earthy with black and brass accents and loads of plants in every corner.

INDOOR PLANTS WERE INCREDIBLY POPULAR IN THE 70S AND IT SEEMS THAT TREND IS WELL AND TRULY BACK. WHY DO YOU THINK THEY'VE HAD SUCH A RESURGENCE?

I guess everyone just got sick of the minimalist trend – I know I did. I think indoor plants have become popular again because people are realising the benefits they bring, especially living in the city. With so much pollution outside it's nice to come home to clean fresh air.

AS A STYLIST YOU'RE CONSTANTLY CREATING BEAUTIFUL IMAGES, HOW DO PLANTS PLAY A ROLE IN SETTING THESE SCENES?

I feel as though a room isn't complete without a natural element and, for me, it's as simple as adding an indoor plant, whether it be a large sculptural plant to add height and depth to a room, or a trailing vine draping from a fireplace or shelf. A touch of greenery instantly removes any clinical vibes a room might give off.

I FEEL AS THOUGH A ROOM ISN'T COMPLETE WITHOUT A NATURAL ELEMENT AND, FOR ME, IT'S AS SIMPLE AS ADDING AN INDOOR PLANT

YOU CHOOSE TO LIVE SURROUNDED BY PLANTS. WHAT EFFECT DO YOU THINK PLANTS CAN HAVE ON OUR SPACES (AND LIVES)?

It's a way to bring literal life into your home, and they make you feel happy and healthy by purifying the air. When I see my plants thriving in my home I know that the environment is healthy, and I know they're keeping the air clean for me in return.

HOW DO YOU KEEP YOUR PLANTS HAPPY AND HEALTHY?

I'm always keeping an eye on them; the light in my house changes quite dramatically from summer to winter, so I need to keep track of how each of them is faring in the space I've placed them. If they're looking a little sad I move them to a new spot near a window and they perk right up. I also give them some liquid seaweed fertiliser once a month so they are able to get extra nutrients. Sun + Love + Water + Music = happy plant = happy me.

WHAT ARE SOME OF YOUR TIPS FOR STYLING YOUR INDOOR PLANTS?

I love to cluster smaller plants in groups and in gorgeous ceramic planters. I like to leave larger plants to stand alone as a sculptural piece.

WHAT'S YOUR FAVOURITE INDOOR PLANT AND WHY?

Oooh, its got be my Monsteras! I have two types and they're both so beautiful and wild. I am very drawn to an earthy colour palette which is quite 70s in itself, so maybe that's why I love the Swiss cheese plant (*Monstera deliciosa*); it was such a popular plant back then.

⌃ UNEVEN GROUPINGS OF PLANTS ARE VISUALLY APPEALING AND SIT PERFECTLY BELOW A WINDOW WHERE THEY ARE CLOSE TO BRIGHT, INDIRECT LIGHT. ⟨ (TOP LEFT) TRAILING PLANTS SUCH AS THE PRETTY CHAIN OF HEARTS FEATURE HEAVILY IN THIS HOME.

^ THERE'S NOTHING LIKE WAKING UP NEXT TO SOME BEAUTIFUL GREENERY AND WITH ALL THAT DETOXIFIED AIR YOU CAN SLEEP EASY WITH YOUR PLANT PALS ABOUT. > A SWISS CHEESE PLANT (*MONSTERA DELICIOSA*) STAKED TO A TOTEM FOR SUPPORT.

SPATHIPHYLLUM
PEACE LILY

While this hardy plant may evoke shopping mall/call-centre vibes, don't discount it just yet. Also known as the 'closet plant' for its ability to grow in very low light, this flowering beauty is one of the easiest houseplants going around, plus it's lush and lovely to boot. While very tolerant of the darker corners of your home, low light can affect the plant's ability to flower, so if it's the bold white flowers that you're after, be sure to give your plant plenty of bright, indirect light.

The Peace lily wears her heart on her sleeve and is pretty good at communicating what she needs. Her leaves will droop when thirsty, but will bounce right back once watered. Leaf tips will go brown if overwatered, and if the leaves become shrivelled and dry you will likely need to give her a good mist to increase the humidity levels.

LIGHT

Low–moderate

WATER

Moderate

SOIL

Well-draining

LIGHT	**WATER**	**SOIL**
Low–moderate	Low	Well-draining

ZAMIOCULCAS ZAMIIFOLIA
ZANZIBAR GEM

For the blackest of black thumbs there really is no going past this tough mofo. It's the Chuck Norris of the plant world. No water, no light, no worries – the Zanzibar gem can roundhouse kick it in some pretty adverse conditions. With its dark-green glossy leaves that unfurl from tuberous roots, this guy is as handsome as he is tough, and adds a much needed splash of greenery without any of the pesky effort. A good watering once a month, and even less in the dormant colder months, is about as taxing as it gets. It's not called the un-killable houseplant for nothing.

CHLOROPHYTUM COMOSUM
SPIDER PLANT

There's nothing creepy or crawly about this indoor gem! The Spider plant is easy-peasy to care for and is prepared to cop plenty of abuse from the most neglectful of owners. It grows happily in a wide range of conditions and it suffers from few problems, apart from occasional brown tips, which can be easily removed. Its name refers to the spider-like plantlets that dangle from the mother plant on suspended branches, like spiders on a web. These miniature versions of the plant are simple to propagate – a perfect and cheap way to grow your plant collection. Spider plants are also praised by NASA for their air purifying abilities – is there anything they can't do?

LIGHT

Bright, indirect

WATER

Moderate

SOIL

Well-draining

LIGHT

Low–moderate

WATER

Moderate. Low in winter for the best blooms

SOIL

Well-draining

HOYA OBOVATA
WAX PLANT

The Hoya gets its name from the man considered responsible for bringing this heavenly species to prominence, botanist Thomas Hoy. Blessed with lush, thick, juicy leaves, it's easy to think of Hoyas as succulents. While there are indeed some succulent Hoyas, the vast majority of them are non-succulent, including this delightful *Hoya obovata*. Referred to as the Wax plant due to its waxy foliage and stems, when it comes to tolerance this beauty reigns supreme. She'll even reward a bit of neglect with some banging blooms, which consist of pretty balls of teeny tiny five-pointed stars that smell as sweet as they look. As if all of this wasn't enough, the Hoya's variegated varieties take this humble plant to a whole new level.

COLOCASIA
ELEPHANT EAR

Luscious large leaves are the name of the game with the aptly dubbed Elephant ear. From the grassiest of greens through to purplish black leaves, this foliage makes one hell of a statement. And don't even get us started on its variegated cousin – a true sight to behold. Be prepared to give this guy some room as it can grow up to 1.2 metres (4 ft) tall. *Colocasia* have a tendency to lay pretty low over winter in a period of dormancy. This can be fairly alarming for the novice gardener, but it's a completely normal part of their growth cycle. Remove any dead foliage and ease up on the watering during this time. Those lovely leaves will be back before you know it.

LIGHT

Bright, indirect

WATER

Moderate–high
+ misting

SOIL

Well-draining,
peat-based

LIGHT

Bright, indirect

WATER

Moderate

SOIL

Well-draining

SYNGONIUM
ARROWHEAD PLANT

Part of the Araceae family, this guy is the *Philodendron's* little brother. Also known as the Arrowhead or Goosefoot plant, it's relatively low maintenance, so you can rest easy and enjoy the greenery or the blush pinkery, depending on the variety. This plant is great for purifying the air in your home. It will creep and crawl if left to its own devices, so regular pruning will help maintain a neater look.

HEUCHERA
ALUMROOT

Sound the bells for this blossoming beauty! Known as both Alumroot, referring to the plant's medicinal roots, and Coral bells for its adorable bell-shaped flowers, this dainty but daring piece of foliage adds some serious pretty to your plant gang. Available in an impressive variety of colours ranging from deep purple to lime green and yellow, you can create you own *Heuchera* rainbow. Generally, bright, indirect light is perfect but some of the darker-leafed varieties can handle a little direct morning sun.

LIGHT

Bright, indirect

WATER

Moderate

SOIL

Moist, well-
draining

LIGHT

Bright, indirect

WATER

Moderate

SOIL

Well-draining

ANTHURIUM
LITTLE BOY PLANT

Also known as the Flamingo flower or Boy flower plant because of its distinctive (and somewhat phallic) flowers, *Anthurium* is resilient and low maintenance. This guy loves bright, indirect light. The lower the light, the less flowers and more foliage you will see, but it's still relatively easy to have the best of both worlds. Just be sure to keep it out of direct sunlight.

   Anthurium is susceptible to root rot so don't overwater and ensure that the soil is well-draining. To promote the best blooms, use a fertiliser that has a high phosphorus number. A feed every few months should do the trick.

EMMA MCPHERSON

Founder of The Plant Room

∧ TIMBER FRAMING IS ADORNED WITH LONG HANGING PLANTS AND VARIEGATED FOLIAGE THAT PROVIDE A VISUAL BREAK BETWEEN DIFFERENT AREAS OF THE OPEN-PLAN SHOP. ❯ HAND PINCHED CERAMICS ADORN A TABLE.

YOUR BACKGROUND IS QUITE DIVERSE, TELL US A BIT ABOUT YOUR PREVIOUS PURSUITS AND HOW YOU CAME TO CREATE THE PLANT ROOM.

My background is really diverse! I spent a lot of years in hospitality and event management, all the while studying things that really interested me, such as metaphysics, parapsychology and astrology. I fell into hospitality when I finished school, but I was always on the hunt for things that helped me understand who I was and what I'm doing here on this crazy planet. After studying everything energetic, I discovered Gestalt therapy which became my world and way of life. I finally left hospitality and became a therapist working with people with addiction. And then I had a baby and everything changed.

My husband and I made a decision to bring up our boy in a household where both parents lived their lives following their bliss and doing what they love every day. Work wasn't work but a way of life that was enjoyable, inspiring and fun. For me, that was design so, once again, I went back to school and studied interior design. I started my own business straight out of college working with residential and commercial clients.

When I began, I was amazed at the lack of plants in people's homes. I grew up with Boston ferns (*Nephrolepis exaltata*) hanging from the ceiling and Monsteras growing up the walls, so to live removed from nature felt very foreign to me and a little hard to comprehend.

The Plant Room was born from a deep desire to create spaces that are sustainable and conscious, filled with soul and the spirit of creation. I grew up in homes with handmade ceramics, timber and plants and, to me, these are the elements that made our house feel like a home. Pieces made from natural materials and created from the heart are filled with the soul of the maker, and I believe something magical happens when you fill your home with these objects. My store is filled with my favourite furniture makers and designers, and everything is made by the hands of someone doing what they love. The pieces hold the spirit of creation and it's this energy and spirit that we then harness for our workshops, collaborations and events.

I GREW UP IN HOMES WITH HANDMADE CERAMICS, TIMBER AND PLANTS AND, TO ME, THESE ARE THE ELEMENTS THAT MADE OUR HOUSE FEEL LIKE A HOME

THE PLANT ROOM IS SO MUCH MORE THAN JUST A PLANT STORE, TELL US ABOUT SOME OF THE AMAZING THINGS YOU GUYS ARE DOING FROM YOUR BEAUTIFUL SPACE.

Yes, The Plant Room is more than a retail store. Depending on the person, this space seems to play different roles in people's lives. For some, it's a place to come and have a chat and a cuppa; for others, it's a place to learn and grow. We are closely aligned with the local community and regularly hold workshops and events. We've held yoga and meditation classes, as well as fibre-art workshops. We've also held events on women's sexuality and we're currently running a series of nights for the LGBTQI kids in our area. We've held talks on everything from body image to how to keep your plants happy. I love that people can come to The Plant Room to explore themselves and what holds meaning to them.

YOU BELIEVE IN THE IMPORTANCE OF LIVING WITH NATURE, HAVE PLANTS ALWAYS PLAYED AN IMPORTANT ROLE IN YOUR LIFE AND SPACES?

Plants have always been a massive part of my life – our houses were filled with them. We always lived surrounded by countryside and I spent most of my days and weekends discovering new waterholes and trees to climb with my friends. I've never really felt removed from nature, so when I moved into design I was quite surprised by the amount of people who do. It makes me wonder what this disconnection does not only to the individual but also, more broadly, to society.

'LIFE IS GROWTH' IS THE TAGLINE ON YOUR WEBSITE, CAN YOU ELABORATE ON THIS IDEA?

I believe in progress and evolution, that we are all here to grow and live in a more conscious way. The Plant Room represents that for me ... everything we do and everything we sell comes from a place of growth. The conversations had, the workshops held, every single thing on the shop floor and shelves are an evolution, a revolution of education and an awakening of consciousness.

I wanted to provide a place that holds the spirit of creation, one that people could walk into and feel connected to both themselves and the environment, a place that we could provide for people to be free from excess and more connected to life, themselves and nature. I surround myself with people and objects that

THERE'S SOMETHING SPECIAL ABOUT THE PAIRING OF A PLANT AND A HANDMADE CERAMIC. EMMA FILLS HER SHOP WITH STUNNING HAND-CRAFTED PRODUCTS THAT ARE PRODUCED WITH SOUL BY THOUGHTFUL MAKERS.

EMMA FEELS AN AMAZINGLY STRONG PULL TO NATURE AND HER SPACE ABSOLUTELY REFLECTS THIS. IT IS A WELCOMING AND
BEAUTIFULLY CURATED STORE WHERE THE RECORDS ARE ALWAYS PLAYING AND THE TEA IS FRESHLY BREWED.

inspire me, but not only that, I hope that other people feel the difference when they walk into The Plant Room. We grow from the conversations we have and how they make us think in new ways – it's the lessons that are learned only by living and seeking something new. Growth can come from heartbreak, or from hard work, but growth happens anyway – it's part of life – so it's important to embrace it, enjoy it and ride the wave.

WE'RE BIG BELIEVERS THAT SPACES ARE ENHANCED BY INDOOR PLANTS. WHAT'S YOUR EXPERIENCE OF LIVING AND WORKING SURROUNDED BY GREENERY?

It inspires me, it's creative, it's passionate, it's open, it's honest and it's real. For me, it's life. We spend so much time living away from nature that I feel lucky to to be surrounded by it on a daily basis. It brings me back to a place of feeling alive, fulfilled and whole. I walk into the store and I feel connected. We might just be talking about a plant and the perfect pot, but there seems to be an energy and connection that exists where the whole is greater than the sum of its parts.

WHAT ARE SOME OF YOUR FAVOURITE INDOOR PLANTS?

That's like asking me to pick a favourite child. There are no favourites. I love nature and I love plants. I always say to my staff if you don't like a plant then there's elements of yourself that you're escaping or avoiding. So, for me, they are just another tool to help me live consciously and learn about myself. Then again, it depends on the area, the light, the space and what a person is wanting out of the plant. They're such amazing beings, and there is always the perfect plant for any environment or occasion.

DO YOU HAVE ANY TIPS FOR THOSE WHO BELIEVE THEY ARE CURSED WITH A BLACK THUMB?

I personally don't believe in black thumbs; for me, everyone has the capacity to connect with their plants. I always suggest that our customers watch and feel their plants and notice the changes. Like people, plants are affected by their environment, water, light, heat and how well they are looked after and cared for. Notice when their colour changes or their leaves start to droop. Treat them like they are part of the family ... dust their leaves, water and feed them. And most importantly, connect – they'll always tell you what they need.

I PERSONALLY DON'T BELIEVE IN BLACK THUMBS; FOR ME, EVERYONE HAS THE CAPACITY TO CONNECT WITH THEIR PLANTS

NEPHROLEPIS EXALTATA

ADIANTUM TENERUM

ADIANTUM RADDIANUM

ASPLENIUM BULBIFERUM

CYRTOMIUM FALCATUM

FERNS

Immortalised by Henri Matisse and um, J.Lo, and praised for their magic air-purifying qualities by none other than NASA, ferns are the perfect addition to your foliage collection. The strapping Boston fern (*Nephrolepis exaltata*) is likely to invoke nostalgic memories of your granny's place, while the dainty and fussy Maidenhair fern (*Adiantum raddainum*) will make you (in the immortal words of Rihanna) work, work, work to see that gorgeous, green mane grow.

LIGHT	WATER	SOIL
Bright, indirect	Moderate + misting	Moisture-retaining

PLATYCERIUM BIFURCATUM

ELKHORN FERN

Elegant and majestic just like its namesake animal, the Elkhorn fern is native to the rainforests of New Guinea and the coast of Queensland. Part of the same family as the Staghorn, they usually grow attached to tree trunks high up in the rainforest canopy. Lucky for you, this epiphyte is just at home in an urban indoor jungle. It needs watering once a week and good drainage is essential – don't let it sit in a puddle of water! Try and mimic the rainforest light by placing your Elkhorn in a lightly shaded area with occasional dappled sunlight.

These clever cookies create their own compost, so don't like to be overfed, especially with artificial fertilisers as they can burn their fronds. You might see the occasional large, brown-felt patches beneath the fronds, but don't stress, these are reproductive spores and, in fact, indicate a happy plant.

LIGHT

Bright, indirect

WATER

Moderate-high
+ misting

SOIL

Moisture-retaining

NEPHROLEPIS EXALTATA

BOSTON FERN

Much loved by the Victorians, this is one of the more dramatic ferns for adding a little pow to your home. Large and leafy, Boston ferns look incredible in a hanging pot or on a stand, allowing their long fronds to elegantly drape down. As far as ferns go, this guy is pretty easy going due to the slightly more robust nature of the foliage. Draughts are still best avoided and a good regular misting will provide the humidity it craves.

LIGHT

Bright, indirect

WATER

Moderate-high
+ misting

SOIL

Moisture-retaining

PTERIS CRETICA
BRAKE FERN

Also known as the Ribbon fern for its long, lanky foliage, these greenies are particularly delightful with their arching stems stretching daintily over a main bed of leaves at the base. As far as ferns go, the Brake fern is one of the easiest to care for and a fairly slow grower that makes for a terrific tabletop plant. They don't enjoy soggy soil, but like their fern cousins they prefer things to be a little on the steamy side.

LIGHT

Bright, indirect

WATER

Moderate
+ misting

SOIL

Moisture-retaining

POLYPODIUM AUREUM
BEAR'S PAW FERN

With furry feet (rhizomes) growing at its base and broader fronds than many of its fern siblings, the common name for this beast will come as no surprise. One of a number of footed ferns that include the Rabbit's foot and Kangaroo ferns, these leafy creatures are slightly out of the ordinary making them a real conversation piece. Their frilly foliage adds to the appeal and provides lovely texture to an indoor jungle.

MAIDENHAIR FERN

Found in rainforests everywhere from Australia to the Andes, there are over 250 species of Maidenhair fern, including the hybrid 'Lady Moxam'. Characterised by light, delicate leaves and a temperamental attitude, this fickle foliage is not for the faint-hearted. Oh so precious, they are very sensitive to changes in light, temperature and humidity. Even a slight breeze can turn this lush fern into a crisp shadow of it's former self. Humidity is key and bathrooms are ideal for providing the conditions needed for these fabulous ferns to thrive.

LIGHT

Bright, indirect

WATER

High + misting

SOIL

Moisture-retaining

JANE WEI

Hair-stylist and owner of A Loft Story

WITH SUCH A LOFTY SPACE, JANE USES HANGING PLANTS AND TALL TREES TO MAXIMISE THE USE OF GREEN. THE LARGE FIDDLE-
LEAF FIG (*FICUS LYRATA*) PICTURED ABOVE TAKES PRIDE OF PLACE IN HER STUDIO.

WE HAVE FOUR
MASSIVE SKYLIGHTS
IN OUR ROOF, PERFECT
FOR PLANTS! I SOURCE
MY SELECTION TO
COMPLEMENT THE
OPEN-PLAN, DOUBLE-
HEIGHT SPACE

—

TELL US A BIT ABOUT YOURSELF: YOUR BACKGROUND, WHAT YOU DO, THE SPACE WE'RE SHOOTING YOU IN.

I've been a hairdresser in Sydney for the last 14 years, and I have always loved being surrounded by plants and nature, art, culture, music and creative people (with good coffee on tap!). When I ventured out on my own and founded A Loft Story, I wanted to incorporate all those elements that inspire me, so I created a working space that not only comprises a ten-chair salon, but also an espresso bar, lots of greenery (not to mention we are across the road from a beautiful park) and art on the walls. There is an amazing group of hairdressers that work here and we are very lucky to be a part of an incredible community, full of creative and inspirational human beings.

YOUR SPACE IS INCREDIBLE. HOW DID YOU GO ABOUT FILLING IT WITH PLANTS?

I am very lucky because we have four massive skylights in our roof, which are perfect for plants! I choose greenery that complements the open-plan, double-height space, along with furniture I've collected. I like to play with the contrasting shapes of the plants. I recently acquired a magnificent 2 metre (6 ft 5 in) wide Staghorn fern that is mounted to the loft balcony 4 metres (13 ft) up, overlooking the entire salon space. Clients can look up and marvel at it while they get their hair washed. I've put Boston ferns in between the basins on top of tree stumps, to create a space barrier between clients and to filter the air for them while their toners get put in.

WHAT IMPACT DO THE PLANTS HAVE ON THE SPACE AND YOUR BUSINESS/WORK?

In the beginning, I wanted to create a hairdressing space with minimum harmful fumes and chaos, and plants are the perfect antidote to this. They filter the air and are such quiet achievers; they literally inspire me in every way. Their existence brings instant relaxation and calmness. Customers and locals love the space and especially the plants!

HAVE PLANTS ALWAYS PLAYED AN IMPORTANT ROLE IN YOUR LIFE?

Well, Green is actually my middle name so it all make sense really! Plants have become more and more of an obsession for me now that I have a huge 240 square metre (2580 square ft) sun-filled warehouse to fill. A Sunday trip to the nursery is my guilty pleasure – I am always on the lookout for the next unique find! Looking at each new baby leaf unfurl or a new flower bloom brings such a sense of accomplishment. Each plant amazes me with its structure and individuality. One of my favourite things to do is to head off into the national parks, mountains and forests on nature-filled adventures on my days off. Plants are my Zen.

WHAT ARE SOME OF YOUR FAVOURITE INDOOR PLANTS AND WHY?

Lately, I am so proud and in awe of my 90 cm (3 ft), lush Donkey's tail. It kicks up its ends like its namesake to tell me it's loving life! My huge Staghorn fern named King George has also got to be up there. Staghorns amaze me with their elegance and alien shapes. I could look at King George for hours on end. And of course, my Fiddle figs, with their huge lush leaves growing from such delicate branches. They are like an elegant ballet dancer, beautiful yet strong.

DRAMTIC FEATURE PLANTS INCLUDING A MASS OF HANGING DEVIL'S IVY (*EPIPREMNUM AUREUM*) THAT COVERS A LARGE
EXPANSE OF WHITE WALL AND A MATURE CONGO (*PHILODENDRON CONGO*) HELP TO LUSH UP THE DOUBLE HEIGHT SPACE.

RHAPIS EXCELSA

LIVISTONA CHINENSIS

PALMS

ARCHONTOPHOENIX ALEXANDRAE

HOWEA FORSTERIANA

These truly tropical beauties bring to mind colonial rooms of the past: ceiling fans lazily lapping at the warm air and green leaves reaching high and wide. Palms had a serious revival in the 70s and have circled right back into fashion today. From the luxe and lovely Kentia (*Howea forsteriana*) to the easy-peasy Parlour palm (*Chamaedorea elegans*), you're spoilt for choice.

LIGHT

Bright, indirect

WATER

Moderate

SOIL

Well-draining

Originating in China, the Rhapis is a palm with many names: Lady palm, Bamboo palm, Fan palm, Finger palm ... just pick your favourite! Her sturdy stems are covered with a fibrous sheath, making the Rhapis palm a tolerant and easy-going addition to your indoor garden. Although slow growing, the fan-shaped leaves can reach heights of 3–4 metres (10–13 ft), but you'll be waiting well over 10 years for that, so as with many indoor plants, patience is a virtue!

RHAPIS EXCELSA

RHAPIS PALM

LIVISTONA CHINENSIS
CHINESE FAN PALM

With broad, you guessed it, fan-shaped leaves of a deep, rich green, the Chinese fan palm is a beautifully architectural plant. Despite it's name, this palm is actually native to Japan's Ryukyu Islands. It prefers warmer climates and is generally easy to manage, growing into a handsome palm that will complement any room you place it in. Treat it right with bright, indirect light and well-draining soil, and this elegant palm will coexist happily in your home for years to come.

LIGHT

Bright, indirect

WATER

Moderate

SOIL

Well-draining

LIGHT
Bright, indirect

WATER
Moderate

SOIL
Well-draining

HOWEA FORSTERIANA

KENTIA PALM

Endemic to Australia's Lord Howe Island, this slow-growing palm requires a bit of nurturing. With a little patience and the right attitude, however, the Kentia will grow to become one of your favourite plant pals. When it comes to re-potting, these guys are the petulant teenagers of the palm family, preferring to be left alone rather than moved from vessel to vessel. The Kentia possesses fragile roots, so if you absolutely have to re-pot, gently does it.

TESS
ROBINSON

Owner and creative director of Smack Bang Designs

TESS HAS A KNACK FOR CURATING AESTHETICALLY PLEASING GROUPS OF GREENERY. HAVING A PARTNER ON HAND WHO IS A TRAINED HORTICULTURALIST ALSO HELPS TESS KEEP HER PLANTS LOOKING HEALTHY AND LUSH.

I THINK IT'S AS SIMPLE
AS PLANTS HELPING
US TO FEEL RELAXED,
AND WHEN WE ARE
TRULY RELAXED
WE HAVE MORE
PSYCHOLOGICAL
BANDWIDTH TO
BE MORE CREATIVE

YOUR BEAUTIFUL STUDIO IS FILLED WITH PLENTY OF PLANT FRIENDS! WE'RE BIG BELIEVERS THAT SPACES ARE ENHANCED BY INDOOR PLANTS, WHAT'S YOUR EXPERIENCE OF WORKING SURROUNDED BY GREENERY?

As an avid plant lady, it was just as critical for us to have a jungle in our studio as it was for us to have working wifi. Even though it takes me a good hour to water them each week, the plants are by far my favourite part of the studio. They help bring the office to life and by bringing the outdoors in, we can almost convince ourselves that we are working outside in the fresh air and sunshine. I have no evidence to prove this, but I'm a strong believer in plants changing the energy of a space making it more conducive to creativity, productivity and happiness – all things which I aspire to cultivate in the Smack Bang Studio on a daily basis.

CREATIVITY IS AT THE HEART OF WHAT YOU GUYS DO AT SMACK BANG; WHAT IMPACT, IF ANY, DO THE PLANTS HAVE ON FOSTERING THAT?

I think it's as simple as plants helping us feel relaxed, and when we're truly relaxed we have more psychological bandwidth to be creative. Humans and plants evolved together, so maybe somewhere deep in our subconscious sharing a space with plants feels more natural and safer than being without them.

FROM A BIT OF INSTAGRAM STALKING WE CAN SEE YOUR PARTNER IS A FELLOW PLANT LOVER. WHAT ROLE DO PLANTS PLAY IN BOTH YOUR LIVES?

Yes, except my partner has taken his obsession one step further and has made it his daily nine-to-five. Our house is completely consumed by plants and we often find ourselves head-over-heels, swooning over photos of our plants like parents would their children. Ridiculous, I know, but they just bring us so much joy.

DO YOU CONSIDER YOURSELF A GREEN THUMB?

Kind of ... but I'm pretty lucky, I get a good head start! My boyfriend is a horticulturalist and expert plant whisperer. So, when my thumb fails me, I take the plant with my tail between my legs and head back to our house to give it a period of respite in Byron's plant hospital. Over the years spent with Byron and running our business, Urban Growers, I have learnt so much about caring for plants. So much so, that I sometimes surprise myself with the plant advice I dish out to friends!

WHAT ARE SOME OF YOUR FAVOURITE INDOOR PLANTS?

My favourite depends on the day! I'm a huge fan of statement plants – anything with an architectural vibe or beautifully shaped leaves. At the moment I'm loving my Lobster claws (*Heliconia*), Fan palms (*Livistona*), and Elephant's ear (*Colocasia*).

WHAT TIPS DO YOU HAVE FOR ADDING PLANTS TO YOUR WORKSPACE? AND KEEPING THEM ALIVE!

1. Where possible, position your greenery close to a window or under skylights to maintain growth and give them a nice view.
2. When it rains, take them outside for a good drenching – I promise you it feels as good for them as it does for us after a three-day festival!
3. If your plants are sitting in air conditioning 365 days a year they are going to need a light misting of water to keep some humidity in the air and the leaves happy. You can do this weekly, and it will also help to deter pests.
4. Re-pot every 1–2 years and only use a premium potting mix. This will ensure your plants get the nutrients they need and maintain good water retention.
5. Don't overwater them! The most common death for indoor plants is drowning. Ensure that they've fully dried out from their last watering session before you water them again.
6. We also love giving our plants a nitrogen-based fertiliser every so often – it keeps them healthy, strong and ultra green.
7. Whisper sweet nothings to them at least once a week.

∧ BIG WINDOWS ARE A REAL PLUS WHEN GROWING PLANTS LIKE THESE BIRD OF PARADISE (*STRELITZIA NICOLAI*) WHICH LOVE
THE LIGHT. PLANTS ARE KNOWN TO INCREASE PRODUCTIVITY AND HAVE CALMING EFFECTS IN OFFICE ENVIRONMENTS.

∧ PLANTS INCLUDING A MOTHER-IN-LAW'S TONGUE (*SANSEVIERIA*) FILL THIS BRIGHT CORNER PROVIDING A VISUAL FEATURE IN A MEETING ROOM > STRING OF BEANS (*SENECIO RADICANS*) GROWING RAMPANT ON THE SUCCULENT-FILLED BALCONY.

PHILODENDRON SELLOUM

PHILODENDRON BIPINNATIFIDUM

PHILODENDRON 'ROJO CONGO'

PHILODENDRON CORDATUM

PHILODENDRON 'XANADU'

PHILODENDRON ERUBESCENS

PHILODENDRONS

As charming as they are varied, Philodendrons can be elegantly feminine, such as the trailing Heartleaf (*Philodendron cordatum*) and vivid Pink princess (*Philodendron erubescens*), to the spiky and sculptural, such as the Xanadu. These hardy and low-maintenance gems are the unsung heroes of many a green gang and remain resplendent in the care of even the blackest-thumbed indoor gardener.

LIGHT

Bright, indirect

WATER

Moderate

SOIL

Well-draining

PHILODENDRON CORDATUM

SWEETHEART PLANT

With the most stunning heart-shaped leaves that trail perfectly from a shelf or plant stand, this pretty piece of foliage is appropriately known as the Sweetheart plant. There's a whole lot to love about this super low-maintenance philodendron. Let it trail or train it to climb across a wall with small hooks. To create fullness, a technique called pinching is helpful. Using your fingernails to pinch, or sharp scissors or secateurs, cut above a leaf node (the place where a leaf is attached to the stem). A new stem will then grow from that node. Don't let those precious cuttings go to waste either; they will root easily in water giving you more sweetheart treasures for your collection.

LIGHT

Bright, indirect

WATER

Low-moderate

SOIL

Well-draining

PHILODENDRON 'ROJO CONGO'
ROJO CONGO

Gardening newbies pay attention, the *Philodendron* 'Rojo congo' is one hardy fella, making it a great starter plant. New leaves emerge a deep, shiny-red colour and grow into bold, oversized green leaves at full maturation. The luscious Rojo congo is a beautiful mid-sized plant suitable for any room, and adds stunning colour to your standard greenery. One of a newer species of non-vining Philodendrons, the Congo is also a gun air purifier so, all in all, it's the perfect house guest.

PHILODENDRON 'XANADU'

XANADU

Good luck thinking of this retro Philodendron without Olivia Newton John's earworm getting stuck in your head! Another of the non-vining Philodendrons (see opposite), the Xanadu will grow wider than it is high, making it perfect for filling an open space. As with most Philodendrons, it's best to keep pets away from these guys as they're mildly toxic when consumed.

LIGHT

Bright, indirect

WATER

Moderate

SOIL

Well-draining

FICUS ELASTICA

FICUS LONGIFOLIA

FICUS LYRATA

FICUS

Arguably the most fashionable of the foliage families, from the glossy and graphic Rubber plant (*Ficus elastica*) to the retro and curvaceous Fiddle-leaf fig (*Ficus lyrata*). Their beauty and popularity knows no bounds, but these stunners are more than just a pretty face. This species plays an essential role in many rainforest ecosystems around the world, as well as in your house-plant collection.

FICUS LYRATA

FIDDLE-LEAF FIG

The supermodel of the plant world, the pretty fiddle's popularity goes from strength to strength. Her voluptuous fiddle-shaped leaves are deliciously retro, but she looks right at home in even the most minimal of settings. She'll make you work for those good looks, though; the *Ficus lyrata* is one demanding diva! It has quite high light requirements, but avoid harsh sun on those precious leaves. Give her a good soaking once a week or so, ensuring that the top 5 cm (2 in) of soil is completely dry before watering again. To help keep foliage growth even, it's a good idea to regularly rotate your plant, as these beauties tend to grow towards the light and can end up a little lop-sided.

LIGHT

Bright, indirect

WATER

Moderate

SOIL

Well-draining

LIGHT

Bright, indirect

WATER

Moderate

SOIL

Well-draining

FICUS LONGIFOLIA
SABRE FIG

The overwhelming popularity of the Fiddle-leaf fig means that some of the more unusual and interesting members of the fig family are sometimes overlooked. With long, thin leaves reminiscent of an Australian native Eucalypt and a tough, robust nature, it's high time *Ficus longifolia* enjoyed its moment in the spotlight. If you're looking for an indoor tree to create a statement in your space, look no further. It's sure to be the next big thing. You heard it here first!

LIGHT

Bright, indirect

WATER

Moderate

SOIL

Well-draining

FICUS ELASTICA

RUBBER PLANT

With robust glossy leaves and the capacity to get nice and big, the Rubber plant is one strapping specimen. There's no question that he's easy on the eye, but these guys are also pretty handy around the house. Those large glossy leaves mean this plant is one of the best in the biz at keeping your space free of nasty toxins. Low maintenance is the Rubber plant's MO, and they will even let a little neglect slide. Keep them thriving with some bright, indirect light and a good water once a week.

To add additional pattern and texture, opt for variegated specimens, such as the Tineke and the Lemon lime variety. Just keep in mind that to maintain the stunning patterning on the foliage, these guys have slightly higher light requirements.

RICHARD UNSWORTH

Landscape designer & founder, Garden Life

RICHARD IS FAMOUS FOR HIS LEAFY FICUS COLLECTION. FROM THE GIANT SABRE FIG (*FICUS LONGIFOLIA*) (SEE PAGE 151), TO THE IMPRESIVE FIDDLE LEAF FIG (*FICUS LYRATA*) PICTURED HERE, HE KNOWS HOW TO KEEP HIS PLANTS HEALTHY AND HAPPY.

I THINK PEOPLE
ARE LOOKING MORE
AND MORE FOR A
REASSURANCE AND
CONNECTION WITH
NATURE, AS OUR URBAN
LIVES BECOME BUSIER

TELL US A BIT ABOUT YOURSELF: YOUR BACKGROUND, WHAT YOU DO, YOUR WORK AND THE SPACE WE'RE SHOOTING YOU IN.

Our store is a destination for lovers of all things garden and green. As well as being garden designers, we source a huge variety of pots, planters and vessels for indoors and outside from all over the world, and bring them together in one huge warehouse space. This is our third store and we've been here two years. We have plenty of room to demonstrate different aesthetics and themes, and people can come and wander, have a coffee and just soak it all up.

INDOOR PLANTS ARE HAVING A MAJOR MOMENT. WHY DO YOU THINK THEY'VE HAD SUCH A RESURGENCE?

I think people are looking more and more for a reassurance and connection with nature, as our urban lives become busier and more disconnected from our roots. Caring for and cultivating indoor plants is rewarding, fulfilling and has proven health benefits – oxygenating the air being only one of them! What's not to love about an indoor tree?

YOU GUYS TRAVEL FAR AND WIDE TO SOURCE INCREDIBLE VESSELS FOR PLANTS. TELL US ABOUT THIS PROCESS AND THE IMPORTANCE OF PICKING THE RIGHT HOME FOR YOUR PLANTS (FROM BOTH A FUNCTIONAL AND AESTHETIC POINT OF VIEW).

Yes, we do travel far and wide to source unique and original pieces – it's something I have always loved doing over the years. I basically design, develop and source items that I love and hope other people will love them also. I love pieces with a history, a story or a strong sense of identity – whether it's an antique Turkish planter, a brass vessel from India or a simple terracotta pot from Morocco, hand-thrown on a traditional foot-wheel.

YOU HELP PEOPLE FILL THEIR HOMES AND OUTDOOR SPACES WITH PLANTS, WOULD IT BE SAFE TO ASSUME YOUR OWN SPACE IS FILLED WITH FOLIAGE?
Funnily enough I only have one indoor plant at home – a big pot of silver Mother-in-law's tongue in my bathroom – but my garden is crammed to the max! I often cut foliage to bring indoors and fill vases; I feel I have enough plants at work.

BE HONEST, FIDDLE-LEAF FIGS (*FICUS LYRATA*) ARE SO UBIQUITOUS THESE DAYS. ARE YOU SUFFERING FROM FIDDLE FATIGUE? WHAT ARE SOME UNDER-RATED ALTERNATIVES PEOPLE COULD TRY INSTEAD?
Haha, fiddle fatigue, I like it. They are such great plants but it's high time their cousins took more of the limelight: try the Rubber plant (*Ficus elastica*) or the Sabre fig (*Ficus longifolia*) – both will turn into indoor trees if you want them to.

WHAT ARE THE BIGGEST MISTAKES PEOPLE MAKE WITH THEIR INDOOR PLANTS? AND WHAT'S YOUR ADVICE FOR KEEPING INDOOR PLANTS HAPPY AND HEALTHY?
You need to choose the right plant for the space you have – it's really all about light and water. If you have a very dark spot, you need something that will cope with that level of light. Also, research what levels of watering your plants require. I often advise people to take their plant outside and drench it, then allow it to dry out in between waterings. I put mine in the shower and they love it.

WHAT'S YOUR FAVOURITE INDOOR PLANT AND WHY?
Ficus longifolia makes such a slender, wispy indoor tree and I love how it adjusts to the light and makes its shape. I have also always loved the simple and classic Cast iron plant (*Aspidistra*). A nice thick healthy specimen in a brass pot looks sensational.

RICHARD COLLECTS AMAZING POTS AND VESSELS FROM ALL OVER THE WORLD. THESE PARTICULARLY BEAUTIFUL GIANT BRASS AND COPPER POTS COME FROM TURKEY AND INDIA, AND SOME WERE ONCE USED TO MAKE CANDY.

PEPEROMIA OBTUSIFOLIA

PEPEROMIA CAPERATA

PEPEROMIA

PEPEROMIA SCANDENS 'VARIEGATA'

PEPEROMIA ARGYREIA

Pretty and petite, these guys may not be the biggest members of your plant gang, but what they lack in size they definitely make up for in fabulous foliage. Although they vary considerably in appearance, these little plant pocket rockets will delight with their fleshy ornamental leaves. From the irresistible Watermelon plant (*Peperomia argyreia*) that will have you dreaming of summer cocktails, to the swoon-worthy trailing Cupid's peperomia (*Peperomia scandens* 'Variegata'), it's time to get on board the Peperomia train.

PEPEROMIA SCANDENS 'VARIEGATA'

CUPID'S PEPEROMIA

With its heart-shaped, trailing green and ivory leaves, this happy guy will bring the Peperomia party into your life and living room. Known as Cupid's peperomia, he will make his way straight into your heart with his seriously low-fuss ways. This plant is perfect for sitting in plant stands or atop shelves in need of some cheering up. Like most of us, he likes a regular drink, but not enough to make him soggy, and a bright spot out of the harsh direct sun.

LIGHT

Bright, indirect

WATER

Moderate

SOIL

Well-draining

LIGHT

Bright, indirect

WATER

Low-moderate

SOIL

Well-draining

PEPEROMIA CAPERATA

EMERALD RIPPLE PEPEROMIA

Hailing from the Brazilian rainforest, the Emerald ripple gets its common name from its deeply corrugated or wrinkled green leaves. With a tough nature and tolerance of fluorescent lights, this low-maintenance beauty makes a fabulous houseplant. It is susceptible to root rot, so ensure that the soil is kept moist, but allowed to drain to avoid soggy feet. A regular dose of half-strength fertiliser in the warmer months will keep this stunner looking its best.

LIGHT

Bright, indirect

WATER

Moderate + misting

SOIL

Well-draining

It's definitely all about the leaves with the Watermelon plant, and it's not hard to guess where the common name of these delightful plants stems from. Their thick, succulent leaves resemble the rind of a watermelon and can grow quite large considering the smallish size of the plant overall – truly a sight to behold! It can take a bit of adjustment to get the water and light requirements right with this guy, so experiment and keep an eye on it until you discover its rhythm. Persevere – it's well worth the effort.

PEPEROMIA ARGYREIA

WATERMELON PLANT

BEGONIA 'IRON CROSS'

BEGONIA SYLVIA

BEGONIA 'BLACK COFFEE'

BEGONIA MACULATA

BEGONIA REX

BEGONIAS

Possessing some seriously fabulous foliage, beautiful Begonias bring whimsy and joy to a plant gang. Colourful and bold, they are grown mainly for their lovely leaves but they also sport delightfully delicate blooms. Pretty as a picture and generally easy to care for, it's time to get acquainted with this charming family of plants.

BEGONIA MACULATA 'WIGHTII'

POLKA DOT BEGONIA

An angel wing (hybrid) begonia, this spotted beauty is a festive and cheerful addition to any indoor jungle. Dramatic silver spots and dainty white flowers are some of Wightii's best features.

Its cane-like stalks have a fairly upright growth habit, but will also sprawl outwards, meaning this plant works equally well in a hanging planter or in a table-top pot. One of the most popular classes of Begonia, the Polka dot is known for its hardiness (and beauty), making it especially suitable for houseplant culture.

LIGHT

Bright, indirect

WATER

Moderate

SOIL

Well-draining

LIGHT

Bright, indirect

WATER

Moderate

SOIL

Well-draining

BEGONIA REX
PAINTED-LEAF BEGONIA

Also referred to as a Fancy-leaf begonia, this guy is known for its showy, graphic foliage. Grown almost exclusively for its large, brightly coloured leaves, its blooms tend to be small and less impressive. This particular variety of Begonia (of which there are hundreds of varieties) is rhizomatous, which means it grows from a thick, fleshy, horizontal underground stem that grows just below the surface of the soil. This stunner likes it nice and humid, but avoid misting the leaves, as it can lead to powdery mildew that will taint that beautiful foliage. Group this plant with other humidity-loving plant pals or sit it on a saucer with pebbles.

The term 'succulent' refers to plants that store water in their leaves and stems, allowing them to withstand periods of drought. The succulent family, which includes *Cacti* and *Euphorbia*, are some of the most varied and interesting collections of plants you can keep indoors. Hailing from exotic desert and jungle regions – from Madagascar to Mexico and well beyond – their often striking and unusual aesthetics make them perfect for adding a bit of quirk to your space. These fascinating and fantastical imports adapt amazingly well to our urban lives, and with the right conditions they will thrive with minimal effort.

Sporting bulbous, juicy leaves and some pretty perfect blooms, succulents are a great option for those of us lucky enough to have a light-filled space. From the sculptural Century plant (*Agave*) to the trailing Donkey's tail (*Sedum morganianum*), these low-maintenance plants add interest and texture, yet ask for little in return. For novice gardeners and those who are a little forgetful on the watering front, they're a good starting point for any plant collection. With so many beautiful varieties out there, you're sure to amass quite a few.

Cacti are differentiated from other succulents by the small bumps or areoles out of which clusters of spines or hairs grow. Helping to protect the plants from predators in

THESE FASCINATING AND FANTASTICAL IMPORTS ADAPT AMAZINGLY WELL TO OUR URBAN LIVES, AND WITH THE RIGHT CONDITIONS THEY WILL THRIVE WITH MINIMAL EFFORT

—

their natural environments, these sometimes deceptively vicious prickles can inflict some pretty nasty pain on unsuspecting and curious observers. When dealing with these spiky suckers, it's important to handle with care!

When most of us think of cacti, it is the quintessential Saguaro cactus standing tall in its desert landscape that often springs to mind. It's less commonly known that a number of cacti are actually native to jungle environments, thus giving rise to two distinct categories with differing light and water requirements.

Desert cacti are by far the larger of the two categories. These sun lovers like things hot and dry, and will thrive best in the brightest areas of your home. Position as close to a light source as possible – a sunny windowsill is ideal. Their ability to hold water in their stems dictates the often bulbous and columnar shape of desert cacti that include well-known species, such as the Golden barrel cactus and Powder puff cactus.

Jungle cacti, as the name so clearly suggests, are native to the rainforests of Central America and Southeast Asia. These mainly epiphytic forest dwellers can often be found trailing from trees below the rainforest canopy, or suspended from rocks where they feed off nutrients from rainwater and nearby decaying plants, including their own dead tissue. They require bright, but dappled light instead of harsh rays that can burn their long succulent stems or branches. With spines that are fairly well hidden, some of the most common jungle cacti include the Mistletoe and Zigzag cactus.

PLANT PEOPLE

CARLY
BUTEUX

Ceramicist and founder of Public Holiday

FROM A SWISS CHEESE PLANT (*MONSTERA DELICIOSA*) TO A SPRAWLING SUCCULENT AND CACTI COLLECTION, EVERY NOOK AND CRANNY OF THIS QUIRKY HOME IS FILLED WITH PLANTS. MANY ARE HOUSED IN CARLY'S OWN HANDMADE CERAMIC VESSELS.

TELL US A BIT ABOUT YOURSELF: YOUR BACKGROUND, WHAT YOU DO, YOUR WORK AND THE SPACES WE'RE SHOOTING YOU IN.

I am currently a one-woman show clay-maker. I spend my days covered in clay making functional ceramic pieces such as mugs, cups and planters. These two hands form every part of my process, from throwing on the wheel to hand painting patterns and glazes. I am really fortunate to have a home studio where I create my work and spend downtime with my partner Joe and our little sausage dog Bam. Our space is an old corner shop that was once upon a time a butchery (as told by our lovely old neighbours). It is a simple but unusual space with concrete floors and plain white walls, which makes it perfect for us to fill with our favourite plants and handmade goods. We were also lucky to have our friend (and superstar artist) Georgia Hill create a giant mural on the outside, which really makes our place that much more special!

AS A MAKER AND CREATIVE, WHAT IMPACT DO PLANTS HAVE ON YOUR WORK AND PRODUCTIVITY?

I think plants have the ability to both foster and stunt productivity! Surrounding yourself with green goodness is the perfect way to make a comfortable and creative work space, encouraging longer and happier days in the studio. That being said, checking on plants, re-potting and propagating can be the perfect way to procrastinate when you're feeling a little restless.

MANY OF YOUR PIECES ARE VESSELS FOR PLANTS, TELL US ABOUT YOUR CERAMICS PRACTICE AND HOW PLANTS ARE CONNECTED WITH THIS.

My ceramics practice has always been instinctively linked to plants and one of the reasons I initially started clay-making was the desire to make homes for my growing plant collection. I think there is something really special about creating a home for a living organism, watching it grow and change shape while sitting inside my work. One of my absolute favourite things is seeing the different pairings people make when they choose plants to live inside my planters. It is magical.

^ A LADDER LEADS TO A LOFT BED MADE BY A FRIEND FROM RECYCLED SCAFFOLDING. IT ALSO DOUBLES AS A PLANT STAND.
‹ SHELVES STACKED WITH CARLY'S GRAPHIC CERAMIC PIECES IN HER HOME WORKSHOP, NOTE OBLIGATORY FOLIAGE TOP RIGHT.

IN OUR FAST-PACED DIGITAL WORLDS, POTTERING AROUND A GARDEN OR CARING FOR AN INDOOR GREEN TRIBE IS THE PERFECT WAY TO GROUND OURSELVES BACK WITH NATURE

BOTH YOUR HOUSE AND STUDIO IS FILLED WITH PLANTS. WHAT EFFECT DO YOU THINK THEY HAVE IN OUR SPACES AND LIVES?

Plants make people happy – I firmly believe that! It is not only the calming effect and fresh air that they bring to our spaces, but also the opportunity to slow the hell down. In our fast-paced digital worlds, pottering around a garden or caring for an indoor green tribe is the perfect way to ground ourselves back with nature. Plants give us the opportunity to nurture, grow and live a peaceful life.

WHAT DO YOU LOVE MOST ABOUT INDOOR PLANTS?

Plants play such a prominent role in our space and, to be honest, we're kind of addicted to the indoor green! There are always new additions to fit in and new homes to accommodate our growing plant friends. Styling our plants allows us to use not only some of my absolute favourite Public Holiday planters (there have been a few that I just couldn't part with!), but also the space around our plants, filled with handmade treasures bought and traded from makers around the globe.

HOW DO YOU KEEP YOUR PLANTS HAPPY AND HEALTHY?

Because we are surrounded by our plants, it's easy to keep a good eye on them. We spend each morning sat in the sun with morning coffees and our favourite records playing. It's the perfect time to check on all our indoor plants and feel if they need watering or a holiday in the back courtyard for a good dose of sun.

WHAT'S YOUR FAVOURITE INDOOR PLANT AND WHY?

What a tough question! How can I choose a favourite when they are all such individuals? I can't go past our spiny cacti collection, or the long dangling arms from our many species of Rhipsalis. I guess one of the plants I have a lot invested in is a small *Monstera obliqua* cutting that was sent to me by Thomas Denning, a horticulture master. It was an unexpected gift which makes it extra special, and I am constantly learning how to create the best conditions to give it a happy life.

^ FOLIAGE PLANTS, SUCCULENTS AND CACTI HAPPILY CO-EXIST AMONG THE BOOKS AND BIKES OF THIS INNER CITY HOME.
< CARLY'S EXTENSIVE SUCCULENT COLLECTION SOAKS UP SOME RAYS IN THE BACK COURTYARD.

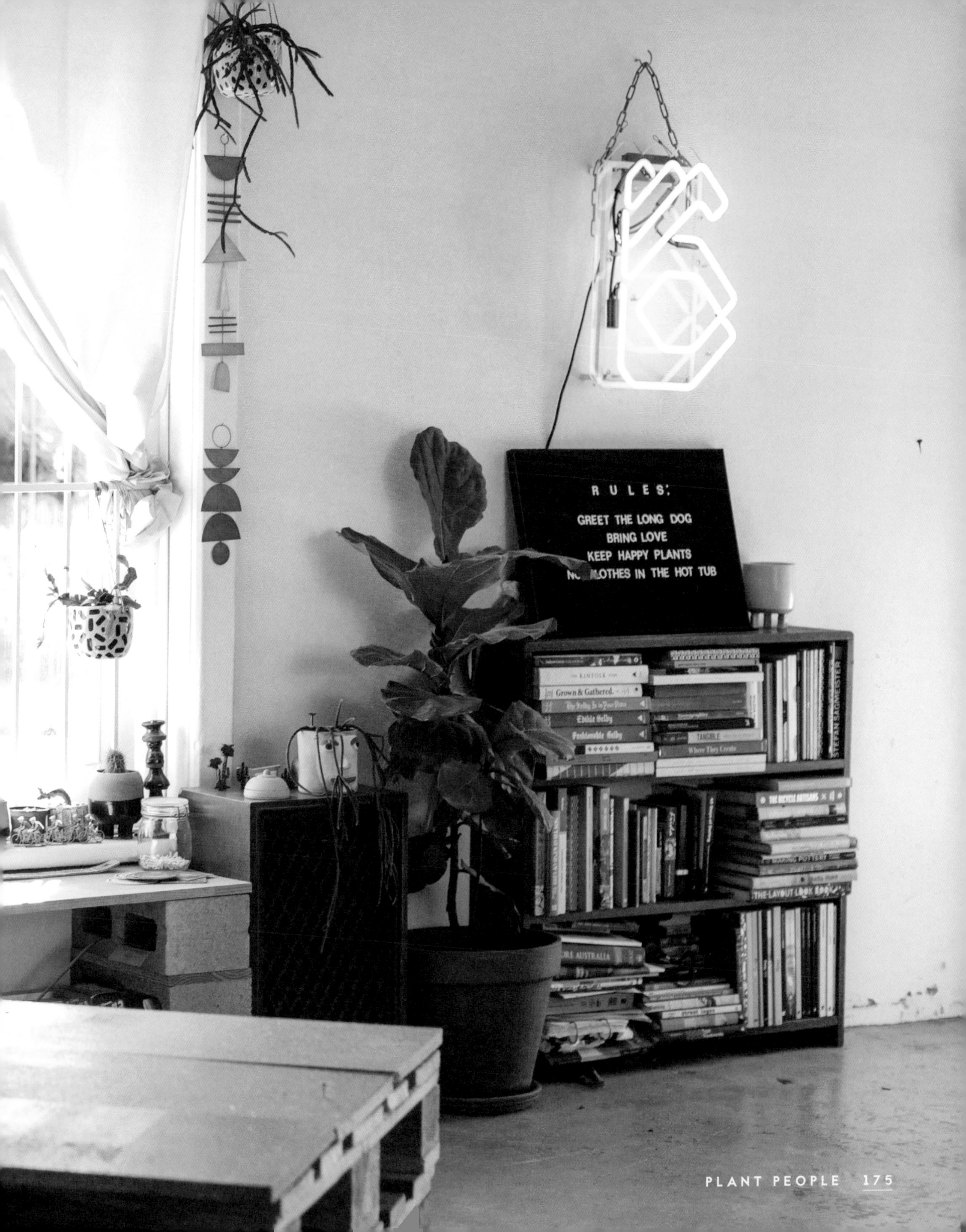

RULES:

GREET THE LONG DOG
BRING LOVE
KEEP HAPPY PLANTS
NO CLOTHES IN THE HOT TUB

SANSEVIERIA 'MOONLIGHT'

AGAVE AMERICANA

KALANCHOE

GASTERIA

SUCCULENTS

EUPHORBIA TRIGONA

SEDUM

GRAPTOVERIA

From the edgy and offbeat African milk tree (*Euphorbia trigona*) to the elegant Mother-in-law's tongue (*Sansevieria*), this varied and adaptable group of plants definitely doesn't succ! With fleshy water-storing leaves and unusual architectural forms, these bad boys are as easy on the eye as they are to care for. Many are effortlessly propagated and will grow rampant in the right conditions, making them the perfect plant choice for the penny-pinching indoor gardener.

LIGHT	**WATER**	**SOIL**
Bright, indirect	Low	Well-draining

CEROPEGIA WOODII

CHAIN OF HEARTS

With the most delicate succulent leaves growing along dainty chains, the pretty Chain of hearts will tug at even the toughest of heartstrings. Their long strands of tiny heart-shaped leaves and cute-as-a-button purple flowers look stunning trailing from a hanging vessel or perched atop a shelf. Bright, indirect light and fortnightly watering will keep your little hearts beating strong. The rarer variegated version is the stunning sister to this succulent.

CENTURY PLANT

If you're the type of person who likes all of the beauty an exotic plant can offer, yet none of the time to make a fuss, then the Agave is for you. They come in myriad shapes and sizes, colours and textures – so the hardest part will be choosing which one to take home! Agave are a rather useful plant, as they are used to make sugar and tequila. The *Agave americana* is, not surprisingly, native to the United States and Mexico, but unlike its more common name suggests, it does not live for 100 years, think closer to 20 or 30. A word of warning: Century plants do have an irritating sap and sometimes very sharp thorns, so they're best kept away from small children and pets.

LIGHT

Bright, direct

WATER

Low

SOIL

Well-draining

LIGHT

Bright, direct

WATER

Low

SOIL

Well-draining

SEDUM MORGANIANUM

GIANT DONKEY'S TAIL

It's the long, succulent-covered stems of this Sedum that gives this plant its common name the Donkey's, or Burro's cactus. This is actually a misnomer as it's not really a cactus, but rather a succulent. Nevertheless, this happy guy is sure to up the texture game in your plant gang. *Sedum morganianum* is a stunning trailing plant with gorgeous green bean-shaped leaves, which are longer and thicker in the giant variety pictured. Flowers emerge in late summer in hanging clusters of small blossoms in red, yellow or white. These guys are perfect on any shelves or plant stands in need of some cheering up.

SANSEVIERIA 'MOONLIGHT'

MOTHER-IN-LAW'S TONGUE

She keeps her opinions to herself and you won't have to tidy up before she arrives. In fact, the Mother-in-law's tongue lights up every room she enters. Her lovely, elongated leaves will brighten up your living spaces and her upright nature makes her the perfect space-saving indoor pal. According to the NASA Clean Air Study, *Sansevieria* has amazing air-purification qualities, removing four of the five commonly found toxins from our spaces. It is also one of the few plants that removes carbon dioxide at night so you can sleep easy. *Sansevieria* is super-low maintenance, making this ol' dame one mother-in-law you'll be more than happy to have around.

LIGHT

Low–moderate

WATER

Low

SOIL

Well-draining

LIGHT	**WATER**	**SOIL**
Bright, indirect	Low	Very well-draining

HAWORTHIOPSIS ATTENUATA

ZEBRA CACTUS

Originating from the Eastern Cape province in South Africa, this petite and super slow-growing succulent is striped perfection. Spiky, graphic and peaking at around 15 cm (6 in) in height, the Zebra cactus is a total cutie and, unsurprisingly, one of the most popular succulent varieties of all. Exotic good looks plus hardiness means these guys make excellent gifts and you'll often find them potted in terrariums or in rows of tea cups on uni students' windowsills.

SENECIO MANDRALISCAE

BLUE CHALK STICKS

The first thing you'll notice about the *Senecio mandraliscae* is its striking colour: an oceanic green-blue that sets this wonderful succulent apart from its more one-dimensional green friends. Often used as a hardy ground cover outdoors, Blue chalk sticks adapt easily to the indoors with little effort required for maintenance. This plant originates from South Africa and, unusually for a succulent, is more dormant in summer, having its growing period in winter. It's easily propagated from cuttings placed into soil, which makes it a lovely plant to share with your friends.

LIGHT

Bright, indirect-direct

WATER

Low

SOIL

Well-draining

LIGHT

Bright, indirect

WATER

Low

SOIL

Well-draining

SENECIO RADICANS

STRING
OF BEANS

If you're not hooked on succulents yet, then this guy will definitely reel you in. Originating from South Africa, *Senecio radicans* is found in both arid deserts and more tropical climes. Commonly known as the String of beans or String of fish-hooks, this plant is an exotic, trailing succulent that even the most black-thumbed among us will have no troubles with. Not only is it easier to care for than its cousin, the String of pearls, this guy is fast growing and will reach the floor before you know it. Interestingly the flowers smell like cinnamon when they bloom in late winter and early spring.

LIGHT

Low–moderate

WATER

Low

SOIL

Well-draining

GASTERIA

OX TONGUE

Not dissimilar in appearance to the humble Aloe, *Gasteria* is a little rarer. This particular fella goes by the slightly unfortunate name of Ox tongue. The species name is also rather regrettably derived from the Latin word for stomach and references the sac-like shape of the flowers. Names aside, this interesting and low-maintenance succer is tolerant of lower-light conditions, making it a resilient houseplant. They actually grow in similar conditions to the Zebra cactus (see page 183), so the two make excellent plant pals.

LIGHT

Bright, indirect

WATER

Moderate

SOIL

Well-draining

AFRICAN MILK TREE

Is it a cactus? Is it a tree? No, it's a Euphorbia! This genus of flowering plant consists of over 2000 species that vary greatly in appearance. From long, tall varieties found in Southern Africa, which mimic the look of cacti, to the unusual, round bowling ball of a plant that is the *Euphorbia obsesa*, these beauties are striking and bold, creating a real conversation piece for your space. Eurphorbias grow naturally in the Americas and tropical Asia, and are also prevalent in southeast Africa and Madagascar. These plants like things light, so be sure to keep them somewhere with bright, but indirect light. They'll need to be watered roughly once a week, and less in the cooler months, but they also don't like it too moist, so make sure the soil dries out thoroughly between waterings. They can be re-potted once a year if you want to see it really grow-grow-grow. Fertilising every few months will also encourage growth.

SEMPERVIVUM ARACHNOIDEUM

COBWEB HENS AND CHICKS

Although you could be forgiven for thinking that these succers are infested with spiders (cue arachnophobic screams), the web formations on this plant are actually hairs that clump across its succulent leaves. An old wive's tale claims that when grown on a roof, they protect the inhabitants from witchcraft and thunderbolts. Unusually, *Sempervivum arachnoideum* originates from the Alps, Apennines and Carpathians, and thus can handle freezing temperatures of -12°C (10°F). On the flip side, they can tolerate heat of up to around 40°C (100°F), making these guys tough as nails.

LIGHT

Bright, indirect

WATER

Low

SOIL

Well-draining

LIGHT

Bright, direct

WATER

Low

SOIL

Well-draining

ECHEVERIA
MEXICAN HENS AND CHICKS

With their ravishing rosette-shaped leaves, this pretty genus is named after the Mexican botanical artist Atanasio Echeverría y Godoy. They like life in the spotlight, so keep it in a spot that's nice and bright. Morning sun is ideal, but be careful with strong afternoon rays that can be a little harsh. Apart from that, these guys aren't ones to make a fuss and are generally low maintenance. Apply water directly to the soil, avoiding the rosette and remove any dead leaves from the base of the plant that can attract pests, such as mealy bugs.

LIGHT

Bright, indirect–
direct

WATER

Low

SOIL

Well-draining

KALANCHOE GASTONIS-BONNIERI
DONKEY EARS

Blessed with beautiful, velvety foliage dotted with spots, this fast-growing succulent's leaves can grow up to an enormous 50 cm (20 in) long and span the size of your hand. It is the shape and texture of this foliage that gives the Kalanchoe it's common name of Donkey ears.

Easy to grow, and even easier on the eye, the flowering varieties are highly enticing with their colourful and long-lasting blooms. These succers prefer bright, sunny locations, such as windowsills, and look fabulous in a pot stand showing off their luscious locks.

Kalanchoe are pretty good at telling you what they need, so get to know the signs: if the top leaves begin to droop your Donkey ears is a little thirsty. Having said that, these guys aren't big drinkers so water fortnightly throughout summer and reduce watering in winter. Let the soil surface dry out between each watering and feed fortnightly in the summer with a liquid or slow-release fertiliser.

Those enticing leaves may look pretty but they're poisonous, so make sure your curious furry friends don't go in for a nibble.

PLANT PEOPLE

KARA
RILEY

Photographer

A BOHEMIAN VIBE PERMEATES KARA'S HOME. A LITTLE COUNTRY COTTAGE SMACK BANG IN THE MIDDLE OF THE CITY FILLED
WITH RETRO KNICK-KNACKS, BOOKS, BEAUTIFUL CERAMICS AND OF COURSE, PLENTY OF PLANTS.

TELL US A BIT ABOUT YOURSELF: YOUR BACKGROUND, WHAT YOU DO, THE SPACE WE'RE SHOOTING YOU IN.

I've taken photographs for a living for the past couple of years, but have always loved photographing life as I see it around me as a way of processing and taking things in. I am an artist at heart, which influences most of what I do, whether that's drawing in my sketchbook, reading and pondering over a good book, or arranging and photographing my houseplants.

I live with my partner Adrien and our dog Willow in an 1870s blacksmith's cottage in Sydney's inner west. I fell in love with our home the minute I saw it – there are so many unique little nooks for plants, and the entire interior is made of beautiful old wood. It reminds me of a country lodge, a tiny little sanctuary among the hustle and bustle.

PLANTS HAVE BEEN A SOURCE OF FASCINATION FOR YOU IN YOUR WORK, WHERE DID THE LOVE AFFAIR START?

When I moved back home after living overseas for a year, I brought back a film camera which I started carrying everywhere, mostly on walks around interesting neighbourhoods in Sydney. I think it was a way of coping with being back, and I started to notice so many beautiful things about my environment, in particular the front gardens of quirky houses and the plants they were filled with. I loved seeing people's plant collections, some neatly thought out and a lot that seemed accidental or thrown together, made up of stolen succulent cuttings and weeds with gorgeous flowers. I became obsessed!

WHY DO YOU LOVE TO PHOTOGRAPH PLANTS SO MUCH?

I love that plants have just as much, if not more, character than a person does, and they always let me take their portrait! I love getting up close and noticing their tiny features – it makes me remember to slow down and just observe. Once I started to become more familiar with different varieties of plants I began noticing them everywhere, even in unexpected places. I love photographing plants that seem out of place and bringing attention to the contrast between urban life and the natural world. Weeds growing in a parking lot can be the most beautiful thing!

> I THINK IT'S AS SIMPLE AS PLANTS HELPING US TO FEEL RELAXED, AND WHEN WE'RE TRULY RELAXED, WE HAVE MORE PSYCHOLOGICAL BANDWIDTH TO BE MORE CREATIVE

YOU'VE FILLED YOUR HOME WITH A GROWING INDOOR JUNGLE. WHAT EFFECT DO YOU THINK PLANTS CAN HAVE IN OUR SPACES AND LIVES?

Plants definitely make me feel happy! They have the power to change the atmosphere of a room completely. There is something so calming about having a bit of nature indoors, especially in the city. I think that everyone could benefit from having at least one house plant to nurture and to admire.

Also, the health benefits are incredible: from houseplants that clean the air in our homes to herbs with amazing healing and medicinal properties.

HOW DO YOU KEEP YOUR PLANTS HAPPY AND HEALTHY?

I like getting to know each plant individually, which involves noticing how frequently they like to be watered, or moving them around to see which position they like best. I give my plants human names according to how I imagine their personalities to be, and have a bit of a chat to each of them when watering.

WHAT ARE SOME OF YOUR TIPS FOR STYLING YOUR INDOOR PLANTS?

Choosing the right container is key! I like finding odd vessels, such as tins or jars from op-shops to use instead of pots, as well as wicker baskets to put around pots. I also love placing cuttings in water and displaying them in clear glass bottles – watching the roots grow is fascinating! In an ideal world, there would be enough natural light to put plants in every corner of the house, but clusters near windows also work well. I have a few plants on little stepping stools or small pieces of furniture near windows to keep them closer to the sun.

WHAT'S YOUR FAVOURITE INDOOR PLANT AND WHY?

My favourite indoor plant is Devil's ivy (*Epipremnum aureum*), especially the variegated kind. It's fairly easy to grow and maintain, and I love that it can hang from the ceiling and creep around the room, appearing larger than it is and filling the space.

THERE'S SOMETHING ABOUT PLANT PEOPLE: THEY'RE OFTEN DOG PEOPLE TOO AND MANY PUPS FIND THEMSELVES WITH PLANT NAMES. HERE'S LITTLE WILLOW PEEKING OUT FROM BEHIND HER FAVOURITE *PHILODENDRON CONGO*.

OPUNTIA MICRODASYS 'RUFIDA'

SELENICEREUS ANTHONYANUS

MAMMILLARIA ELONGATA

CACTI

Spiky, sculptural and with a dry sense of humour, these guys are a real winner for those prone to forgetting to water their plants. From round orbs such as the Golden barrel cactus (*Echinocactus grusonii*) to the long, thin arms of the Starfish cactus (*Stapelia grandiflora*), there are endless varieties to choose from. Or why not get one of each? Yes, they can inflict pain, but their spikes are useful in defending against would-be plant predators, and their flowers will be the make-up kiss you were hoping for.

STAPELIA GRANDIFLORA

ECHINOCACTUS GRUSONII

MAMMILLARIA BOCASANA

LIGHT

Bright, indirect

WATER

Low

SOIL

Well-draining

SELENICEREUS ANTHONYANUS

FISHBONE CACTUS

With a silhouette to die for, the Fishbone or Zigzag cactus is so named because of it's graphic saw-like foliage. It also has the benefit of being easy to maintain, making it a great addition to any living space. The epiphytic *Selenicereus anthonyanus* does occasionally flower, but only at night and only for 24 hours, so keep your wits about you when you see it in bud. They look great grouped with other trailing foliage or as an individual hanging plant, and are extremely hardy. Watch out for some pretty nasty spines hidden in the inner ridges of the leaves – we learnt that the hard way!

LIGHT

Bright, indirect

WATER

Moderate

SOIL

Sandy + coarse

ECHINOCACTUS GRUSONII
GOLDEN BARREL CACTUS

Named for its golden ribs and spines, the *Echinocactus grusonii*, or Golden barrel cactus, is one of the easiest cacti to keep indoors. Hailing from the deserts of the southern USA and Mexico, they prefer a hot and dry climate. Once planted in decent cacti potting mix, they're virtually a set-and-forget plant pal. These guys can live for up to 30 years and are slow growers, but persistence will pay off as they start to flower after 20 years! Keeping your Golden barrel away from humidity and ensuring that they have good drainage is the key to keeping these guys happy. Don't allow them to sit in water or leave any water sitting in their pot base, or they will end up with a bad case of root rot.

LIGHT

Low–moderate

WATER

Low

SOIL

Well-draining

With a 'do resembling Robert Smith of The Cure and a preference for the darker corners of your home, the Mistletoe cactus might just be the wonderfully decorative green goth your space needs.

The Mistletoe loves humid conditions, so they're a great addition to your bathroom. Alternatively, they make a cute desk buddy if you're craving a bit of green in your windowless cubicle. It will need watering, but like all cacti it hates to sit in the wet. Being a jungle cacti direct sun is too harsh for the succulent strands of this little plant, so keep it in a spot that receives only moderate, indirect light.

RHIPSALIS BACCIFERA

MISTLETOE CACTUS

GEORGINA REID

Founder and editor, The Planthunter

GEORGINA ENCOURAGES THE MOST UNTAMED, NATURAL GROWTH IN HER PLANTS. THEY'RE A BIT LIKE HER, EARTHY AND WILD. THE ECLECTIC COLLECTION OF GREENERY GIVES HER WAREHOUSE STUDIO A RUSTIC JUNGLE FEEL.

IF PLANTS DON'T EXIST,
WE DON'T EXIST.
THAT'S ENOUGH OF
AN IMPETUS TO LIVE
A LIFE SURROUNDED
BY PLANTS, RIGHT?

THE PLANTHUNTER EXPLORES THE RELATIONSHIP BETWEEN PLANTS AND PEOPLE. HOW DO PEOPLE BENEFIT FROM HAVING A LIFE FILLED WITH PLANTS?
The bonds between people and plants, while often hard to articulate or quantify, run incredibly deep. Firstly, if plants don't exist, we don't exist. That's enough of an impetus to live a life surrounded by plants, right? Secondly, tending to plants teaches so many lessons about the intricate connections between all life. The poet Stanley Kunitz once wrote, 'The universe is a continuous web, touch it at any point and the whole web quivers.' I love this sentence, because it illustrates both the incredible beauty and fragility of existence, and the interconnectedness of all life. Plants, and the act of gardening, teach us about life and perspective in a way few other pursuits can.

ON THE FLIP SIDE, DO PLANTS BENEFIT FROM BEING AROUND PEOPLE?
I guess it depends on context. An indoor plant needs people otherwise it'll die a long, slow death due to starvation. But people, clearly, are not always good for plants. I imagine the millions of trees that have lived for centuries – standing tall and silent in forests, along rivers, in bushlands – that've been razed to the ground as a result of mindless human desires. They clearly haven't benefitted from being around people.

WHAT ARE SOME OF YOUR FAVOURITE INDOOR PLANTS?
I love Hoyas. They're subtle and beautiful and tough. Then there's Rhipsalis – I've got plenty of them. And Lepismium, Peperomia and more. I love them all, and have an ever-revolving collection hanging out in my living room and kitchen.

WHAT'S YOUR NUMBER ONE TIP FOR KEEPING INDOOR PLANTS HEALTHY?

Don't overwater your plants! Remember that life inside is tough for plants and that there's actually no such thing as an indoor plant. Plants that survive indoors are just more tolerant of low light and harsh conditions than others. Take them outside for a holiday every now and again, or if you can't do that, stick 'em in the shower!

DO YOU THINK THAT PLANTS INSPIRE YOU CREATIVELY? CAN YOU DISCUSS THIS PROCESS?

Of course they do! I've always loved and been inspired by plants and nature. As a child this meant pressing flowers and helping my mum in the garden. As an adult it's meant designing gardens for others, writing about plants and creativity, and launching The Planthunter. Plants are very much a part of who I am; they are my muse.

STANDING PROUDLY ON THE STAIRWAY TO HEAVEN, GEORGINA HAS AN AMAZING COLLECTION OF FERNS, BEGONIAS, PHILODENDRONS, RHIPSALIS, PLANT BOOKS AND EVEN SOME DRAMATIC PAMPAS GRASS-SEED HEADS.

STAPELIA GRANDIFLORA
STARFISH CACTUS

Beautiful, but a little hard on the nose, this fast-growing, upright succulent has developed an interesting technique to attract insects. Similar in some respects to carnivorous plants (but not actually meat-eaters), their spectacular flowers emit the stench of rotten meat, which encourages flies to land and pollinate. It's best to enjoy the spectacle of their blooms from a safe distance! So, popping your Starfish cactus on a high shelf when it's flowering is a good idea. Although generally low maintenance, Stapelia are susceptible to pests in their roots so ensure that the soil is very well-draining and water with a good systemic insecticide, added as needed. In winter, hold off watering altogether.

LIGHT

Bright, indirect - direct

WATER

Low

SOIL

Sandy + coarse

LIGHT

Bright, indirect

WATER

Low

SOIL

Sandy + coarse

MAMMILLARIA BOCASANA
POWDER PUFF CACTI

A super-sweet species of cacti with over 200 varieties, you'll have no trouble finding the right Mammillaria for you. Hailing from the deserts of southwest USA and Mexico, these low-growing barrel-shaped cacti are a care-free addition to your indoor garden. Pretty and petite, they grow anywhere from 1–40 cm (½–16 in) tall and 1–20 cm (½–8 in) wide. In addition to their delightful shape, they produce a beautiful crown of pink or purple flowers, capping off what is a wonderful little cactus. Suspending watering during the depths of winter will encourage those beautiful blooms.

LIGHT	**WATER**	**SOIL**
Bright, indirect-direct	Low	Sandy + coarse

OPUNTIA MICRODASYS

BUNNY EARS CACTUS

With their perfect little bunny ear-shaped pads and super-easy-to-care-for attitude, these cuties are a perfect addition to any houseplant collection. But be warned! These guys are armed and dangerous with prickles thinner than the finest human hairs that come off in large numbers upon the slightest touch. They can cause some pretty nasty skin irritation, so approach with caution. Fertilise your Bunny ears with diluted houseplant food or a cactus formula every other time you water it during spring and summer. Occasionally, the plant will be harassed by pests, such as mealybugs and scale insects. These can be dealt with by removing the offending bugs with a cotton bud dipped in alcohol. You should also re-pot your little bunny every one to two years. In addition, these plants can be easily propagated by simply removing one of its succulent pads and allowing the end to dry out slightly for a few days before popping it in some cactus and succulent potting mix. Wait at least one to two weeks before starting a regular watering schedule to give it some time to root. Once established, water infrequently and only water lightly every three to four weeks – seriously, no more – in autumn and winter.

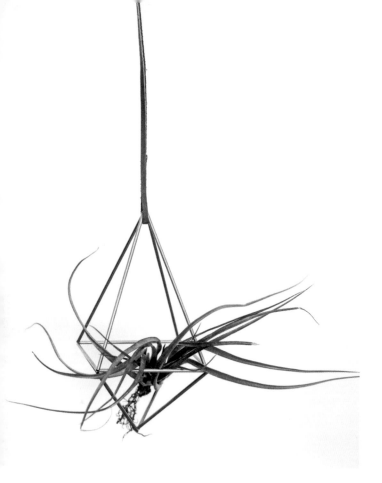

There are a number of plants that don't neatly fit into the other categories listed in this book, but are still worthy of some special attention. The plants in this chapter are some of the harder-to-find and more interesting houseplants, for those on the hunt for something a little out of the ordinary.

There's something undeniably intriguing about plants that can survive without soil, but air plants (*Tillandsia*) can do just that. They are epiphytes, meaning they live by attaching themselves to other plants (or rocks or human-made structures), sourcing their nutrients from the air, water and debris found close by. They enjoy a harmonious, symbiotic relationship with their plant host that is beneficial to both parties.

Without the confinement of a pot filled with soil, the possibilities for displaying these curious plants are endless. Whether suspended from the finest of fishing wire to create an almost floating indoor garden, or perched atop a wire stand, your space is sure to benefit from the addition of these graphic and fascinating beauties.

Carnivorous monsters are also featured here, as they are not your run-of-the-mill houseplants and can certainly take a little more effort to get your hands on. Like orchid thieving, finding and growing a gang of carnivorous plants can quickly become an addiction and before you know it, your home will be bursting with them. Forewarned is forearmed!

You only have to look at social media to see the insane popularity of the Chinese money plant (*Pilea peperomioides*). We feel it deserves a special callout, not only for being hard to get your hands on, but also for its beautiful backstory. Originating in China, this pretty plant made its way to Scandinavia and beyond through simple acts of kindness. It is said that Norwegian missionary Agnar Espegren, brought it back from China to Norway in 1946. Travelling throughout the country on his return, Agnar gifted shoots of the plant to friends, effectively distributing the plant in his homeland, where it is now widely displayed as a windowsill plant, and where it is commonly known as the Missionary plant.

The collecting of unusual plants can quickly turn into an obsession, and you'll soon be scouring nurseries, the internet and garage sales searching for that elusive prize. It's a rewarding moment when you first lay your hands on one of these rarities and have it sitting pride of place in your collection, so let the hunt begin!

THE COLLECTING OF UNUSUAL PLANTS CAN QUICKLY TURN INTO AN OBSESSION, AND YOU'LL SOON BE SCOURING NURSERIES, THE INTERNET AND GARAGE SALES SEARCHING FOR THAT ELUSIVE PRIZE

AIR PLANTS

Stylish and super easy to care for (these guys don't even need soil), air plants are a fun and unusual addition to your plant gang. Air plants come in may fascinating forms, from Spanish moss, which pours from old trees in the American South to crazy, twisting Giant tillandsia. They are native to the southern United States, Mexico, Central and South America, and are part of the Bromeliad family.

There are a few different ways to water your air plants. The most common is to soak them in water for varying amounts of time and regularity (see the following pages for more information). There is also a quicker, dunking method. Whichever you use, it's important to tip your plants upside down and gently shake off excess water before allowing them to dry out completely (ideally overnight to avoid plant rot) and returning them to their home. Be sure to water your new air plant the day it arrives, as it may have dried out a little in transit. You can also mist them in between waterings, if it's particularly hot. Something to note is that they don't enjoy chlorinated water, so let your tap water sit for 24 hours before using it to soak or mist your plants.

Air plants enjoy a breeze, so it's important to keep them in a well-ventilated environment. As a general rule, greener air plants tend to dry out faster, while their more silver brothers and sisters are more drought tolerant.

Happy air plants will flower intermittently – just be sure to gently cut the flower off once it has died. They will also breed little pups. Once these pups have reached half the size of their parent they can be gently detached to live by themselves – it's that simple!

Air plants look great hanging in any contraption, and they also look sweet sitting in pots (just remember to omit the soil), gathered in groups or just chilling solo on your coffee table or shelf.

There are more than 650 types of air plants, so we've selected a few of our favourites to get you inspired to add these fascinating little guys to your collection.

TILLANDSIA XEROGRAPHICA IS ONE OF OUR ALL-TIME FAVOURITE SPECIES OF AIR PLANTS.

LIGHT

Bright, direct

WATER

High

SOIL

Moisture-retaining

SARRACENIA
PITCHER PLANT

These carnivorous creatures are truly a sight to behold. With their tubular trumpets, beautiful colours and tall, delicate flowers, they always make us think of *Day of the Triffids*. Native to the United States and Canada, they grow in boggy areas. Their nectar, scent and colouring attract insects who become trapped and then drown in the base of the pitcher. The plant releases a digestive fluid, which aids decomposition of the insect whose nutrients (nitrogen and phosphorus) are then absorbed by the plant. It's best to prune dead foliage to keep your plant looking trim, and fill its saucer with a bit of water in addition to regular watering, to help keep the soil moist. They're incredibly fascinating plants that we're sure you'll get hooked on.

LIGHT	**WATER**	**SOIL**
Bright, indirect	Moderate	Well-draining

PILEA PEPEROMIOIDES

CHINESE MONEY PLANT

The popular but elusive *Pilea peperomioides* is flooding Pinterest boards around the world. And while they can be hard to track down, it really is worth the hunt! This petite plant may only reach heights of around 30 cm (12 in), but the striking, round leaves – reminiscent of pancakes – are the reason it is so loved, and where its other common name, the Pancake plant, derives. One of the nicest qualities of this plant is that it is very easily propagated and shared with your plant-loving friends. Little pups will begin to grow from the base of the plant. Once these are at least 5 cm (2 in) high, simply cut with a clean knife and place in water or moist soil. They should root within six weeks.

A couple of tips: rotate your plant so it doesn't grow unevenly and make sure it doesn't sit in its own water, as it is prone to root rot.

TILLANDSIA BRACHYCAULOS

TILLANDSIA XEROGRAPHICA

TILLANDSIA IONANTHA

AIR PLANTS

TILLANDSIA STREPTOPHYLLA

TILLANDSIA STRICTA

Plants that don't need soil sound like a crazy anomaly but with the ability to survive on little more than water, air and old plant matter, these intriguing critters are a magnificent example of the power of plants. As epiphytes, air plants enjoy a harmonious relationship with the plant or structure to which they attach themselves, meaning they're just as at home in the nook of a big old gum tree as they are in the hip brass himmeli hanging from your curtain rail.

LIGHT

Bright, indirect

WATER

Mist regularly

SOIL

None, but keep
well-ventilated

TILLANDSIA USNEOIDES

SPANISH MOSS

Tillandsia usneoides is one of the most prevalent air plants available. Going by the names Spanish moss, Old man's beard or Tree hair, it's not difficult to tell what these little guys are going to look like. Divinely draped from tree branches in its native environment, and just as happy trailing from a hook or the top of a bookshelf in your home, Spanish moss provides maximum impact for very little effort. Without the need for soil, what Spanish moss really appreciates is regular misting, good airflow and a breeze to sway in.

LIGHT

Bright, indirect-direct

WATER

Soak fortnightly for 15 minutes, mist regularly

SOIL

None, but keep well-ventilated

TILLANDSIA XEROGRAPHICA

GIANT TILLANDSIA

With bold silvery leaves that start wide and taper out into a curled rosette, the Giant tillandsia is a stunning addition to any plant collection. Growing larger than many of their Tillandsia cousins, these guys look wonderful peeking out from a hanging pot or draping over the corner of a shelf. Another fabulous feature is that they flower for a reasonably long period, giving you ample time to admire their lovely pink and purple blooms.

LIGHT	**WATER**	**SOIL**
Bright, indirect	Soak for 30 minutes once a week + misting	None, but keep well-ventilated

TILLANDSIA IONANTHA

SKY PLANT

This little guy is native to Central America and Mexico. The *Tillandsia ionantha* begins its life with silvery-green foliage, which slowly turns into a stunning pinkish-red when it enters its bloom cycle. Soon afterwards, a purple shoot with delicate, golden floral tips will emerge, perfectly crowning this stunning little plant. They make an awesome feature in any space, and do really well hanging solo, or among a little jungle of indoor plants. You can buy great mini hanging air-plant holders, or get creative and make your own out of driftwood, wire or string.

TILLANDSIA STRICTA

TILLYS

In the wild, these tough hombres can grow as well in sand dunes as they do on trees making them one of the more hardy varieties of air plant around. *Tillandsia stricta* bloom in summer with striking pink leaves and delicate purple flowers. Although they only flower for a short period, the colourful leaves that emerge prior to flowering will last for up to three months. Afterwards, blooming pups will grow, so keep an eye on them and separate them once they've reached a mature size.

LIGHT

Bright, indirect

WATER

Soak 1–2 times a week for 30 minutes

SOIL

None, but keep well-ventilated

LIGHT

Bright, indirect

WATER

Dunk in water once
every few weeks,
mist infrequently

SOIL

None, but keep
well-ventilated

TILLANDSIA STREPTOPHYLLA
SHIRLEY TEMPLE

Named after the child star for its curly head of locks, this is one tangled and terrific air plant. These beauties hail from the wilds of southern Mexico, Guatemala and Honduras, where they are pollinated by hummingbirds and bats. They will flower pink and purple bursts that add another dimension to their beauty. *Tillandsia streptophylla* prefer drier conditions than your average air plant, so are happier with a good dunking rather than soaking.

PLANT PEOPLE

JIN
AHN

Co-founder, Conservatory Archives

WHEN YOU WALK INTO CONSERVATORY ARCHIVES YOUR SENSES ARE CONFRONTED BY THE MASS OF GREENERY COVERING
EVERY SURFACE. FROM THE GROUND TO THE TOP OF THE DOUBLE-HEIGHT CEILING, IT'S AN IMPRESSIVE GREEN OASIS.

TELL US A BIT ABOUT YOURSELF: YOUR BACKGROUND, WHAT YOU DO, THE SPACE WE'RE SHOOTING YOU IN.

I was born and raised in Seoul, the most crowded city in the world. I moved to the UK in 2010 to improve my English skills and make a change from my career as a fashion designer.

Spending time in the English countryside was inspiring. I come from a huge city with a lot of concrete. I thought, if I can work with nature, I'll live happily ever after, so I decided to study horticulture.

While I imagined I'd be working in a botanical garden or a nursery, the reality of working outside in the English weather wasn't ideal for this city girl. After completing my degree and moving to London, I realised I could use my previous experience and background in design and business to open a store dedicated to indoor gardening in the context of a big city, and so Conservatory Archives was born.

HOW DID YOU COME TO OPEN CONSERVATORY ARCHIVES AND WHAT IS IT ALL ABOUT?

Once I had finished my degree it seemed weird to me that people gave little attention to indoor gardening, and not many stores and businesses in London specialised in indoor plants. Seoul has a very different lifestyle than here, as the majority of people live in high-rise buildings, which means no outdoor gardens. So I grew up seeing loads of houseplants. The creative locals in East London are very supportive of what we are doing so it seems we made the right choice.

HOW HAS YOUR DESIGN BACKGROUND INFLUENCED YOUR WORK WITH PLANTS?

My background in design, as well as growing up in the city, means I feel very comfortable with interior spaces. I like to see plants in buildings, surrounded by furniture and other things. My interest in design and vintage furniture definitely influenced the idea of what Conservatory Archives would be as well as the look and feel of the store itself. I believe choosing a plant is not dissimilar to choosing a piece of furniture, so why not do both in the same place?

I THOUGHT, IF I CAN WORK WITH NATURE, I'LL LIVE HAPPILY EVER AFTER, SO STUDYING HORTICULTURE SEEMED LIKE A GOOD FIT!

HAVE PLANTS ALWAYS PLAYED AN IMPORTANT ROLE IN YOUR LIFE?

My mum has always been really into indoor gardening. She loves succulents and our apartment in Seoul was full of them. But it wasn't until I took time away from my career in the UK that I thought about plants becoming a job. Being away from the hustle and bustle of Seoul and spending time in nature, I started to realise the importance of a connection to the natural world, especially for urban-dwellers.

WHAT ARE SOME OF YOUR FAVOURITE INDOOR PLANTS AND WHY?

There are too many to mention. I like plants with lots of branches, as they look like sculptures. When helping people to choose a plant I like to encourage them to think about the level of light in their space as well as the kind of lifestyle they live. If you have a windowsill that gets a good amount of natural light, small succulents are easy to start with – they may forgive you for a month of neglect (so do not overwater!).

CO-FOUNDERS JIN AND GIACOMO LOVINGLY TEND TO THE MASSIVE NUMBER OF PLANT BABIES IN THEIR EAST LONDON STORE. WATERING IS ONE HELL OF A JOB WITH THAT MUCH GREENERY TO CARE FOR!

A SMALL SELECTION OF THE MANY FOLIAGE PLANTS AND SUCCULENTS ENJOYING THE DAPPLED MORNING LIGHT THROUGH
THE FRONT WINDOWS OF CONSERVATOY ARCHIVES IN LONDON'S EAST.

ABOUT

Leaf Supply is the love child of two friends and massive plant nerds, Lauren Camilleri, a magazine art director and indoor plant specialist who owns online plant and design store Domus Botanica, and Sophia Kaplan, the plant and floral stylist of her namesake business Sophia Kaplan Plants & Flowers, and founder of the blog The Secret Garden.

'We get our kicks from early-morning markets and sourcing the healthiest, sexiest greens at secret nurseries. We collab' with local ceramicists, makers and design creatives to come up with unique pots and accessories that give interiors addicts the tingles. We think life just feels better surrounded by living green goodies. So we started Leaf Supply to share the love.'

Lauren Camilleri My parents have always been keen gardeners and they've kept adding to and evolving a really beautiful garden in our family backyard. Having always lived in apartments since leaving home I, too, wanted to have my own oasis of green to nurture and enjoy. Easier said than done.

Having killed more succulents than I'd care to admit, I bought a gorgeous little *Monstera deliciosa*. I was determined to keep this beautiful plant alive; no more horticultural failures destined for the bin. I began to research how to care for indoor plants and realised that with a few simple techniques I could spare my plant buddy from a similar fate to those that had gone before it. Not only did it survive, it grew! I loved seeing it thrive in the corner of my tiny living room. With each new leaf I became more confident that my black thumb could be turned green and from that beautiful little Monstera I started on the journey to grow my indoor jungle.

GREEN-THUMB SKILL: With a degree in interior architecture, graphic design in her bones and a love for foliage, Lauren lives for matching the right plant with the right nook, where it can live its best life. Her addiction to ceramics is a sickness.

SPIRIT PLANT: *Monstera deliciosa* (aka Swiss cheese plant). Those graphic, glossy leaves are a designer's dream. But it's definitely not a case of style over substance with this beauty, as they're also robust and delightfully low maintenance.

Sophia Kaplan I always looked forward to visiting my Nonno, as he would inevitably put us to work in his garden. He had a real passion for growing things he could eat, including a giant macadamia tree in the middle of the yard. I've always enjoyed getting among the dirt and find gardening incredibly therapeutic. Watching things grow, and nature do it's weird and wonderful thing is just so joyous. I try to surround myself with plants as much as possible. Tending to my patch in a local community garden as well as filling my home with indoor green satisfies a desire to connect with nature daily.

GREEN-THUMB SKILL: Growing and styling plants has become a full-time job for Sophia, who also works with flowers to create wild natural scenes for her clients. She loves nurturing creative partnerships as well as finding unusual varieties of plants for all the leaf lovers out there.

SPIRIT PLANT: Pitcher plants (*Nepenthes*). These intensely beautiful and other-worldy plants quickly become a collector's obsession.

THANKS

WHEN WE STARTED LEAF SUPPLY WE SET OUT TO CREATE A COMMUNITY OF PLANT LOVERS AND THIS BOOK IS TESTAMENT TO THAT

WHEN SOMEONE OFFERS YOU the opportunity to create a book, it's not the kind of thing you turn down. We're so grateful to Paul McNally for giving us the chance to share the Leaf Supply love in printed form. A big thank you to Lucy for whipping our ramblings into shape and helping us craft a cohesive and hopefully useful guide to living with indoor plants.

When we started Leaf Supply we set out to create a community of plant lovers and this book is testament to that. We absolutely couldn't have done it without the amazing generosity of the following bunch of like-minded foliage fiends: Emma McPherson, Tahnee Carroll, Kara Riley, Richard Unsworth, Tess Robinson, Georgina Reid, Carly Buteux and Joe Dodd, Jin Ahn and Giacomo Plazzotta, Jane Wei and Jardine Hansen. We loved being welcomed into your lush spaces and imparted with such vivid experiences of living with your own indoor jungles.

To our amazing growers, you slave away in those greenhouses to cultivate and nurture the most beautiful plants, many of which appear on these pages. The extensive knowledge shared over cups of tea in the nurseries has been inspiring and totally invaluable.

Creating a book is definitely a combined effort of many fabulous people: shout-outs to our friends and families, most notably our partners Anthony and Michael who have put up with us while we wrote, scheduled, sourced, shot and designed, and our parents Maree, Richard, Janice and Lewis for all they have done to help support Leaf Supply and our many other endeavours. For those who helped by reading and editing, being photographed, lending us their homes and studios, we are super thankful.

But perhaps most importantly we need to send a huge boom-pow to absolute legend and photographer extraordinaire, Luisa Brimble. Her enthusiasm right from the word go has been unwavering and her stunning images that capture the plants, spaces and people so perfectly are the backbone of this tome. We can't wait to keep creating beautiful plant-filled images with you!

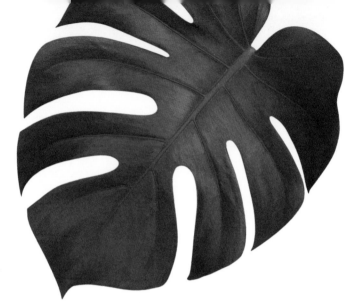

Smith Street Books

PUBLISHED IN 2018 BY SMITH STREET BOOKS
MELBOURNE | AUSTRALIA
SMITHSTREETBOOKS.COM

ISBN: 978-1-925418-63-7

CIP DATA IS AVAILABLE FROM THE NATIONAL LIBRARY OF AUSTRALIA

PUBLISHER: PAUL MCNALLY
SENIOR EDITOR: LUCY HEAVER, TUSK STUDIO
DESIGN CONCEPT + LAYOUT: LAUREN CAMILLERI
PHOTOGRAPHER: LUISA BRIMBLE
ADDITIONAL PHOTOGRAPHY: PAGE 47 BY TOMMY THOMS,
CONSERVATORY ARCHIVES ON PAGES 17, 27, 31, 39, 51, 221,
235-241, 244, 249 BY ANNA BATCHELOR

THANK YOU TO COUNTRY ROAD, GRAFA, WORKTONES AND
TARA BURKE FOR KINDLY LENDING PROPS THAT FEATURED IN THIS
BOOK. WE ALSO ACKNOWLEDGE THE LEGENDS AT THE GLUE
SOCIETY WHO GENEROUSLY ALLOWED US TO SHOOT IN THIER
INCREDIBLE PHOTOGRAPHY STUDIO.

PRINTED & BOUND IN CHINA BY C&C OFFSET PRINTING CO., LTD.
BOOK 53
10 9 8 7 6